30-MINUTE
SUPPERS

10 9 8 7 6 5

First published in 2011 by BBC Books, an imprint of Ebury Publishing
A Random House Group company. This revised edition published 2014.

Photographs © BBC Worldwide 2011
Recipes © BBC Worldwide 2011
Book design © Woodlands Books Ltd 2014
All recipes contained in this book first appeared in BBC Good Food magazine.

The Random House Group Limited Reg. No. 954009

Addresses for companies within the Random House Group can be found at www.randomhouse.co.uk

A CIP catalogue record for this book is available from the British Library

The Random House Group Limited supports the Forest Stewardship Council® (FSC®), the leading
international forest-certification organisation. Our books carrying the FSC label are printed on FSC®-
certified paper. FSC is the only forest-certification scheme supported by the leading environmental
organisations, including Greenpeace. Our paper procurement policy can be found at
www.randomhouse.co.uk/environment

To buy books by your favourite authors and register for offers visit www.randomhouse.co.uk

Printed and bound in China by Leo Paper Products Ltd.
Colour origination by Dot Gradations Ltd, UK

Edited by Barney Desmazery
Commissioning Editor: Lizzy Gray
Project Editor: Lizzy Gaisford
Designers: Interstate Creative Partners Ltd
Design Manager: Kathryn Gammon
Production: Alex Goddard
Picture Researcher: Gabby Harrington

ISBN: 9781849908702

MIX
Paper from
responsible sources
FSC® C018179

PICTURE CREDITS

BBC Good Food magazine and BBC Books would like to thank the following people for providing photos. While every effort has
been made to trace and acknowledge all photographers, we should like to apologise should there be any errors or omissions.

Will Heap p163, p175; Adrian Lawrence p29, p117, p201; Gareth Morgans p41, p55, p57, p61, p63, p73, p105, p115, p147, p153,
p199, p205, p211; David Munns p19, p21, p23, p67, p85, p87, p89, p91, p95, p103, p123, p131, p141, p143, p145, p159, p161, p165,
p195, p207; Myles New p27, p31, p33, p39, p43, p45, p65, p69, p75, p83, p93, p101, p109, p111, p135, p137, p139, p173, p179,
p181, p183, p187, p197, p209; Lis Parsons p11, p13, p15, p25, p35, p37, p47, p53, p59, p71, p77, p79, p81, p119, p121, p125, p127,
p129, p133, p155, p169, p171, p185, p189, p191, p193; Howard Shooter p97; Sam Stowell p17, p49, p51, p99, p107, p149; Rob
Streeter p113; Yuki Sugiura p167; Philip Webb p151, p157, p177

All the recipes in this book were created by the editorial team at Good Food and by regular contributors to BBC Magazines.

BBC goodfood

30-MINUTE SUPPERS

Editor **Sarah Cook**

BBC
BOOKS

Contents

Introduction

· · · · · · · · · · · · · · · · · · · ·

Good food doesn't have to take ages to prepare and cook. Sometimes the best dishes are the quickest and easiest to prepare. Revised and updated with fresh new recipes and a brand new look, this edition proves that quick and easy can also mean hearty and delicious.

Think you can't eat healthily and quickly? You're wrong, and we've got lots of superhealthy ideas to prove it. Plus meat-free options to keep vegetarians happy, and plenty of curries, stir-frys and pizzas that take less time to knock up than it would take you to pick up a takeaway. We've also added a few puddings, to satisfy a sweet tooth when time is tight, so whether you're a busy mum with hungry mouths to feed, want something on the table quick, or are looking to impress guests with little effort, you'll find something to suit you in this collection of 101 recipes.

Even better, these are all favourites from the team at *Good Food* magazine, so you can rest assured they'll work first time and every time. And by including a few of our trademark tricks and some clever uses of ingredients, we make the most of the time you've got to spend in the kitchen, however short that is.

So put down that ready meal, drop the takeaway menu and set the clock – because in 30 minutes or less you'll have dinner on the table.

Sarah

Sarah Cook
BBC *Good Food* Magazine

Notes &
Conversion Tables

· · · · · · · · · · · · · · · · · · · ·

NOTES ON THE RECIPES
- Eggs are large in the UK and Australia and extra large in America unless stated.
- Wash fresh produce before preparation.
- Recipes contain nutritional analyses for 'sugar', which means the total sugar content including all natural sugars in the ingredients, unless otherwise stated.

OVEN TEMPERATURES

GAS	°C	°C FAN	°F	OVEN TEMP.
¼	110	90	225	Very cool
½	120	100	250	Very cool
1	140	120	275	Cool or slow
2	150	130	300	Cool or slow
3	160	140	325	Warm
4	180	160	350	Moderate
5	190	170	375	Moderately hot
6	200	180	400	Fairly hot
7	220	200	425	Hot
8	230	210	450	Very hot
9	240	220	475	Very hot

APPROXIMATE WEIGHT CONVERSIONS
- All the recipes in this book list both imperial and metric measurements. Conversions are approximate and have been rounded up or down. Follow one set of measurements only; do not mix the two.
- Cup measurements, which are used in Australia and America, have not been listed here as they vary from ingredient to ingredient. Kitchen scales should be used to measure dry/solid ingredients.

Good Food is concerned about sustainable sourcing and animal welfare. Where possible, humanely reared meats, sustainably caught fish (see fishonline.org for further information from the Marine Conservation Society) and free-range chickens and eggs are used when recipes are originally tested.

SPOON MEASURES

Spoon measurements are level unless otherwise specified.

- 1 teaspoon (tsp) = 5ml
- 1 tablespoon (tbsp) = 15ml
- 1 Australian tablespoon = 20ml (cooks in Australia should measure 3 teaspoons where 1 tablespoon is specified in a recipe)

APPROXIMATE LIQUID CONVERSIONS

METRIC	IMPERIAL	AUS	US
50ml	2fl oz	¼ cup	¼ cup
125ml	4fl oz	½ cup	½ cup
175ml	6fl oz	¾ cup	¾ cup
225ml	8fl oz	1 cup	1 cup
300ml	10fl oz/½ pint	½ pint	1¼ cups
450ml	16fl oz	2 cups	2 cups/1 pint
600ml	20fl oz/1 pint	1 pint	2½ cups
1 litre	35fl oz/1¾ pints	1¾ pints	1 quart

One-pan prawn pad Thai

A simple version of the Thai classic – serve it with sweet chilli sauce and prawn crackers, plus a sprinkling of chopped, roasted peanuts, if you like.

🕐 30 minutes   🍽 4

- 200g/8oz rice noodles
- 200g/8oz raw peeled king prawns
- 1 tsp finely chopped or grated ginger
- 2 tbsp sunflower oil
- 4 eggs, beaten
- 100g/4oz beansprouts
- 4 baby pak choi or 1 small young cabbage, shredded
- 6 spring onions, thinly sliced
- 1 tsp soy sauce

1 Pour a kettleful of boiling water over the noodles and cover for 10 minutes. Meanwhile, mix together the prawns and ginger. Heat 1 teaspoon of the oil in a large non-stick frying pan and stir-fry the gingery prawns over a high heat for 2 minutes until pink. Tip into a bowl.

2 Return the pan to the heat and add a tablespoon of the oil. When hot, pour in the beaten eggs, spreading them out to form an even layer. Cook until set, then lift out of the pan, roughly shred with a knife and set aside. Drain the noodles.

3 Heat the remaining oil in the pan and stir-fry the beansprouts, pak choi or cabbage and spring onions for 2 minutes or until the pak choi softens. Return the prawns, noodles and eggs to the pan and add the soy sauce, tossing to combine. Serve immediately.

PER SERVING 362 kcals, protein 21g, carbs 44g, fat 13g, sat fat 3g, fibre 1g, sugar 2g, salt 0.82g

Spiced lamb & coconut pilaf

This quick one-pot needs no accompaniments, and if you're not keen on lamb simply swap it for minced beef or pork.

 30 minutes   4

- 1 tbsp olive oil
- 1 onion, finely chopped
- 500g/1lb 2oz lean minced lamb
- 350g/12oz basmati rice
- 2 tbsp Thai green curry paste
- 300ml/½ pint hot chicken stock
- 400ml can reduced-fat coconut milk
- 140g/5oz frozen peas
- 1 lemon, cut into wedges
- handful coriander leaves, to garnish

1 Heat the oil in a pan and cook the onion for 3–5 minutes until soft. Add the lamb and stir-fry for 5–7 minutes until it turns brown.

2 Stir in the rice, curry paste, stock and coconut milk. Bring to the boil, then turn down the heat and simmer very gently for 10–12 minutes until the rice is tender and the liquid has mostly been absorbed.

3 Stir in the peas, cook for 2 minutes more, then squeeze over the lemon, sprinkle over the coriander and serve.

PER SERVING 709 kcals, protein 36g, carbs 79g, fat 31g, sat fat 18g, fibre 4g, sugar 5g, salt 1.21g

Prawn & coconut laksa

Much more substantial than a bowl of soup, a bowl of laksa makes a quick supper for one.

 20 minutes | 1

- 2 tsp oil
- 1 garlic clove, crushed
- 1 spring onion, finely chopped
- 2 tsp finely chopped ginger
- 1 green chilli, deseeded and finely chopped
- juice ½ lime
- 100g/4oz raw peeled prawns (any size)
- 165ml can coconut milk
- 100ml/4fl oz chicken or vegetable stock
- 100g/4oz dried egg noodles
- chopped coriander, to garnish

1 Heat the oil in a large pan or wok. When hot, throw in the garlic, spring onion, ginger and chilli. Cook on a medium heat for 3–4 minutes, then squeeze in the lime juice.

2 Stir in the prawns, then add the coconut milk and stock. Simmer gently for 5 minutes on a low heat until the prawns are pink.

3 Meanwhile, cook your egg noodles in a pan of boiling water for 4 minutes until soft. Drain, then tip into the laksa pan. Season to taste, then serve in a bowl, topped with coriander.

PER SERVING 823 kcals, protein 33g, carbs 79g, fat 44g, sat fat 25g, fibre 3g, sugar 7g, salt 2.19g

Sichuan-style pork & green bean stir fry

. . . .

The Sichuan pepper adds an authentic flavour to this quick supper, but if you can't find it you can use readily available Chinese five-spice instead.

🕐 30 minutes 🍽 2

- 100g/4oz basmati rice
- 200g/8oz green beans, topped and tailed, then halved
- 1½ tbsp sunflower oil
- 140g/5oz minced pork
- 4 tsp dark soy sauce
- 2 tsp rice wine
- 1 tsp caster sugar
- ¼ tsp Sichuan pepper, lightly crushed using a pestle and mortar
- 1 red chilli, halved and sliced
- 4 fat garlic cloves, finely chopped
- 1 small knob ginger, peeled and finely chopped
- 3 spring onions, 2 finely chopped,1 sliced to serve
- 2 tsp sesame oil

1 Cook the rice according to the pack instructions. In a separate pan, boil the beans for 4 minutes, then drain under cold water, pat dry and set aside.

2 In a large non-stick wok or frying pan, heat 1 tablespoon of the oil. Add the minced pork and fry for a few minutes, breaking it up into small pieces with the back of a spoon. Stir in half the soy, the rice wine and sugar, and cook for 30 seconds more. When the meat is cooked through, tip on to a plate.

3 Heat the remaining oil in the wok or pan. Add the pepper, chilli, garlic, ginger and chopped spring onions, and stir-fry for 2 minutes until the ginger and garlic have softened. Tip in the beans, heat through, then add the mince – stir-fry for 2 minutes until hot. Stir in the rest of the soy and the sesame oil. Scatter with the sliced spring onion and serve with the rice.

. . . .
PER SERVING 447 kcals, protein 20g, carbs 48g, fat 19g, sat fat 4g, fibre 6g, sugar 6g, salt 2g

Chicken chow mein

You won't need salt and pepper to season this dish, but you can add an extra splash of soy sauce, if you prefer a saltier flavour.

🕐 25 minutes   🥧 4

- 3 garlic cloves, crushed
- finger-sized knob ginger, grated
- 1 red chilli, deseeded and chopped
- 1 tbsp soy sauce
- 2 tbsp tomato purée
- 2 chicken breasts, cut into chunky strips
- 3 blocks dried egg noodles
- ½ broccoli head, broken into florets
- 3 carrots, cut into thin sticks
- 1 tbsp vegetable oil
- 300g pack beansprouts
- 3 spring onions, halved and sliced into strips
- 1 tbsp oyster sauce

1 Mix together the garlic, ginger, chilli, soy sauce and tomato purée, then add the chicken and leave to marinate while you prepare the rest of the ingredients.

2 Boil a large pan of water, add the noodles, broccoli and carrots, then cook for 4 minutes before draining.

3 Heat the oil in a wok, tip in the chicken and its marinade, then stir-fry for 4–5 minutes until cooked. Toss in the noodles, vegetables, beansprouts and spring onions to warm through. Mix the oyster sauce with 2 tablespoons water and stir this in just before serving.

PER SERVING 545 kcals, protein 33g, carbs 80g, fat 12g, sat fat 1g, fibre 7g, sugar 12g, salt 1.98g

Prawn, pea & tomato curry

You can reach for seconds of this delicious curry – low in fat, it also provides three of your 5-a-day.

 20 minutes 4

- 1 tbsp vegetable oil
- 2 onions, halved, each cut into 6 wedges
- 6 ripe tomatoes, each cut into 8 wedges
- finger-sized knob ginger, chopped
- 6 garlic cloves, roughly chopped
- 3 tbsp curry paste (try tikka masala)
- 400g/14oz raw peeled king prawns
- 250g/9oz frozen peas
- small bunch coriander, leaves chopped, to garnish
- basmati rice or chapattis, to serve

1 Heat the oil in a frying pan, then fry the onions over a medium heat until soft and beginning to brown, about 5 minutes. Meanwhile, reserve eight of the tomato wedges, then whizz the remainder in a food processor along with the ginger and garlic.

2 Add the curry paste to the pan and heat for 30 seconds. Stir through the tomato mix and remaining tomato wedges, then bubble over a high heat for 5 minutes, stirring so the sauce doesn't catch. Mix in the prawns and peas; simmer until the prawns are pink and cooked through. Scatter with coriander, then serve with rice or chapattis.

PER SERVING 236 kcals, protein 24g, carbs 18g, fat 8g, sat fat 1g, fibre 6g, sugar 10g, salt 1.24g

Potato & chorizo pizza breads

· · · · · · · · · · · · · · · · · · · ·

These low-fat crispy pizzas are inspired by a popular German snack – try swapping the chorizo for ham or salami.

 20 minutes 4

- 3 medium–large potatoes, very thinly sliced
- 4 wholemeal tortillas
- 6 tbsp half-fat crème fraîche
- ½ onion, thinly sliced
- 8 thin slices chorizo from a pack, diced
- 25g/1oz mature Cheddar, grated
- 3 tomatoes, roughly chopped
- 2 tsp balsamic dressing
- ½ x 50g bag rocket leaves

1 Heat oven to 200C/180C fan/gas 6. Bring a pan of water to the boil, then blanch the potato slices in it for 2 minutes until almost cooked. Drain well, then tip on to kitchen paper to dry.

2 Put the tortillas on to baking sheets. Season the crème fraîche, then spread over the tortillas. Top with the potato slices, onion and chorizo, then scatter over the grated cheese.

3 Bake for 8 minutes until crisp and golden. Meanwhile, mix the tomatoes with the dressing and ½ teaspoon coarsely ground black pepper, then toss through the rocket. Pile a quarter of the salad in the middle of each tortilla and serve straight away.

· ·

PER PIZZA 287 kcals, protein 11g, carbs 37g, fat 12g, sat fat 5g, fibre 5g, sugar 5g, salt 1.01g

Lamb, lemon & dill souvlaki

Try varying the lamb with chicken, pork, beef or prawns – just remember to adjust the cooking times accordingly.

 30 minutes 4

- 2 garlic cloves, finely chopped
- 2 tsp sea salt
- 4 tbsp olive oil
- zest and juice 1 lemon
- 1 tbsp finely chopped dill
- 700g/1lb 9oz lean lamb, such as neck fillet or boneless leg, trimmed, then cut into large chunks
- pitta or flatbreads, plus salad and tzatziki (optional), to serve

1 Pound the garlic with the sea salt in a pestle and mortar (or use a small food processor) until the garlic forms a paste. Whisk together the oil, lemon juice and zest, dill and garlic salt, then mix half of this with the lamb and combine well.

2 Thread the meat on to pre-soaked wooden or metal skewers. Heat grill to high or have a hot griddle pan or barbecue ready. Cook the skewers for about 2–3 minutes on each side, basting with the remaining marinade. Heat the pitta or flatbreads briefly, then stuff with the souvlaki. Add salad and tzatziki, if you like.

PER SERVING 457 kcals, protein 34g, carbs none, fat 35g, sat fat 14g, fibre none, sugar none, salt 0.27g

Sweet & sour pork stir fry

A quick classic for two, plus this time it's also low in fat. Just add egg noodles or rice to serve.

🕐 15 minutes   🥧 2

- 227g can pineapple slices in juice, drained and chopped, juice reserved
- 1 tbsp cornflour
- 1 tbsp tomato sauce
- 1 tsp soy sauce
- 1 tsp brown sugar
- 2½ tbsp rice wine vinegar or white wine vinegar
- 1 tbsp sunflower oil
- 200g/8oz stir-fry pork strips, trimmed of fat
- 1 red pepper, deseeded and cut into chunks
- 3 spring onions, quartered and shredded
- rice or egg noodles, to serve

1 Mix 4 tablespoons of the reserved pineapple juice into the cornflour until smooth then stir in the tomato and soy sauces, sugar and vinegar. Set aside.

2 Heat the oil until very hot in a wok, then throw in the pork for 1 minute, stirring. Lift the pork out on to a plate, then set aside.

3 Add the pepper to the wok, stir-fry for 2 minutes, then add the pineapple and most of the spring onions for 30 seconds. Stir in the sauce for 1 minute, splashing in a little water as it cooks, then stir the pork back in for 20–30 seconds until just cooked through – it should still be tender. Scatter with the remaining spring onions and serve with rice or noodles.

PER SERVING 284 kcals, protein 24g, carbs 31g, fat 8g, sat fat 2g, fibre 2g, sugar 24g, salt 0.96g

Chicken-teriyaki skewers with griddled spring onions

The same marinade would work equally well with pork, beef or chunks of salmon – simply adjust the cooking time according to the ingredient.

🕐 30 minutes 🍴 4

- 2 tbsp clear honey
- 75ml/2½fl oz teriyaki sauce
- 1 tbsp soy sauce
- 4 chicken breasts, cut into chunks
- bunch spring onions, trimmed
- 1 tbsp vegetable oil

1 If using wooden skewers, soak them in water for 20 minutes to prevent them burning. Heat grill to high and line a baking sheet with foil.

2 Mix together the honey and teriyaki and soy sauces in a bowl. Add the chicken pieces and mix to coat. Thread the chicken on to the skewers. Put on the lined baking sheet and cook under the grill for about 15 minutes until charred, turning and basting them with any sauce from time to time. Check that the chicken is cooked through before serving.

3 Meanwhile, heat a griddle pan until hot. Toss the spring onions in the oil and some seasoning, tip into the pan and cook for 3–4 minutes until nicely charred and softened. Serve with the chicken skewers.

PER SERVING 190 kcals, protein 31g, carbs 7g, fat 4g, sat fat 1g, fibre none, sugar 7g, salt 2.5g

Indian mince with fresh tomato salad

A fragrant twist on beans on toast – swap the lentils for a can of beans, if you prefer.
If you're feeding vegetarians, the beef is easily swapped for veggie mince.

 20 minutes   4

- 1 red onion, sliced
- 300g/10oz minced beef
- 2 tbsp medium or mild curry powder
- 700ml/1¼ pint hot beef stock
- 3 tomatoes
- handful coriander leaves
- 4 mini naans
- 1 x 400g can Puy lentils, drained and rinsed

1 In a non-stick frying pan, dry-fry the onion and mince over a high heat for 2 minutes, breaking up the mince as you go. Stir in the curry powder, pour in the stock, then fiercely simmer for about 10 minutes.

2 While the mince is cooking, dice the tomatoes and roughly chop the coriander, then mix together in a small bowl. Put the naans briefly in a toaster until warmed through, then pop each one on a plate.

3 Stir the lentils into the mince and heat through for a minute, then spoon a quarter of the mince over each naan and top with a spoonful of the fresh tomato and coriander salad.

PER SERVING 417 kcals, protein 28g, carbs 40g, fat 17g, sat fat 7g, fibre 8g, sugar 6g, salt 2.1g

Egg-fried rice with prawns & peas

This Chinese take-away favourite is a great way to use up leftovers – add diced leftover chicken or bacon and a handful of shredded greens for an extra bite.

🕐 25 minutes   🥧 4

- 250g/9oz basmati rice
- 2 tbsp vegetable oil
- 2 garlic cloves, finely chopped
- 1 red chilli, deseeded and shredded
- 2 eggs, beaten
- 200g/8oz frozen peas
- 1 bunch spring onions, finely sliced
- 250g/9oz small cooked and peeled prawns
- 1 tbsp soy sauce, plus extra for serving (optional)

1 Put the rice in a pan with 600ml/1 pint water. Bring to the boil, cover, then simmer for 10 minutes or until almost all the water has gone. Leave off the heat, covered, for 5 minutes more.

2 Heat the oil in wok or large frying pan. Add the garlic and chilli, then cook for 10 seconds – making sure it doesn't burn. Throw in the cooked rice, stir-fry for 1 minute, then push to the side of the pan. Pour the eggs into the empty side of the pan, then scramble them, stirring. Once just set, stir the peas and spring onions into the rice and egg, then cook for 2 minutes until the peas are tender. Add the prawns and soy sauce, heat through, then serve with extra soy sauce on the side, if you like.

PER SERVING 407 kcals, protein 26g, carbs 56g, fat 10g, sat fat 2g, fibre 4g, sugar 2g, salt 1.9g

Pitta pizzas

Easily doubled to feed a family – kids will enjoy eating and helping you make these speedy favourites.

 20 minutes  2 Easily doubled

- 4 wholewheat pittas
- 4 tsp sun-dried tomato purée
- 3 ripe plum tomatoes, diced
- 1 shallot, thinly sliced
- 85g/3oz chorizo, diced
- 50g/2oz mature Cheddar, grated
- few basil leaves, to garnish (optional)
- green salad, to serve

1 Heat oven to 200C/180C fan/gas 6 and put a baking sheet inside to heat up. Spread each pitta with 1 teaspoon of the purée. Top with the tomatoes, shallot, chorizo and Cheddar. Put on the hot sheet and bake for 10 minutes until the pittas are crisp, the cheese has melted and the chorizo has frazzled edges.
2 Scatter with basil, if you like, and serve with a green salad.

PER SERVING 565 kcals, protein 29g, carbs 61g, fat 25g, sat fat 10g, fibre 8g, sugar 9g, salt 3.56g

Thai beef salad

For the best-tasting steak, cook the meat from room temperature rather than fridge-cold.

 20 minutes 2

- 300g/10oz rump steak, fat trimmed
- 2 tsp groundnut oil
- juice 1 lime
- 1 red chilli, deseeded and sliced (bird's-eye chillies work well)
- 1 tbsp light soft brown sugar
- 85g bag baby leaf salad
- 140g/5oz beansprouts
- 140g/5oz red grapes, halved
- cooked rice, to serve (optional)

1 Rub the steak with 1 teaspoon of the oil and season. Fry in a hot pan for 2–2½ minutes on each side (depending on thickness), for medium–rare. Transfer to a plate, cover loosely with foil and rest for 5 minutes.

2 Make the dressing by mixing together the lime juice, chilli, sugar and remaining oil in a bowl. Set aside until the sugar has dissolved.

3 Divide the salad leaves, beansprouts and grapes between two serving bowls. Thinly slice the steak and add the juices to the dressing. Drizzle this over the salads, toss with the sliced beef and serve immediately with rice, if you like.

PER SERVING 317 kcals, protein 36g, carbs 21g, fat 11g, sat fat 3g, fibre 2g, sugar 19g, salt 0.25g

Aubergine & black bean stir fry

· ·

This substantial stir fry is great for vegetarians (just make sure the sauce you use is suitable). Add some chunks of tofu, if you want to increase the protein.

🕐 30 minutes 🍴 4

- 250g/9oz basmati rice
- 4 tbsp groundnut or vegetable oil
- 2 large aubergines, cut into quarters and then wedges
- 2 red peppers, deseeded and cut into thin strips
- 8 spring onions, 7 quartered lengthways, 1 finely sliced
- 220g jar black bean sauce

1 Cook the rice according to the pack instructions. Meanwhile, heat a wok and add the oil. When hot, stir-fry the aubergines for 10–12 minutes until golden and cooked through. Add the peppers and quartered spring onions, and stir-fry for about 6 minutes until just tender.

2 Add the black bean sauce along with 2 tablespoons water and warm through. Serve with the basmati rice and the finely sliced spring onion.

· ·

PER SERVING 411 kcals, protein 11g, carbs 65g, fat 14g, sat fat 2g, fibre 7g, sugar 14g, salt 3.53g

Minty lamb flatbreads

· ·

This Turkish-style supper is super-easy. If you like your food spicy add a chopped chilli in with the garlic.

 25 minutes   4

- 400g/14oz lean minced lamb
- 1 garlic clove, crushed
- 1 tsp ground cumin
- 2 tsp ground coriander
- 2 handfuls mint leaves, half chopped
- 2 large tomatoes, deseeded and diced
- 4 small khobez flatbreads or 4 soft flour tortillas
- 4 tbsp low-fat natural yogurt

1 Cook the lamb mince for 5–6 minutes in a non-stick frying pan over a high heat. When starting to brown, stir in the garlic and spices, then cook for 2–3 minutes more until the mince is brown and there is no liquid left in the pan. Stir in the chopped mint, tomatoes and some seasoning.

2 Heat grill to high. Arrange the flatbreads or tortillas on a baking sheet and spread the mince mixture over them. Grill for 2–3 minutes. To serve, scatter over the whole mint leaves and drizzle with yogurt.

· ·

PER FLATBREAD 355 kcals, protein 25g, carbs 26g, fat 17g, sat fat 7g, fibre 2g, sugar 4g, salt 0.86g

Honey & sesame beef noodles

· ·

Sesame seeds add texture and flavour to a stir fry; add a splash of sesame oil, too, if you have some in the cupboard.

🕐 25 minutes   🍽 2

- 100g/4oz wholewheat noodles
- 2 tsp sunflower oil
- 125g pack purple sprouting broccoli (or Tenderstem), cut into short lengths
- 100g/4oz sugar snap peas, halved
- 4 spring onions, cut into short lengths
- 2 tbsp reduced-salt soy sauce
- 175g/6oz lean rump steak, thinly sliced
- 2 tsp sesame seeds
- 2 tbsp clear honey

1 Cook the noodles in boiling salted water until just tender, then drain and rinse in cold water. Heat half the oil in a non-stick wok. Add the broccoli, peas and 2 tablespoons water, then cover and steam-fry for 3 minutes. Remove the lid, add the spring onions and stir-fry for 2 minutes, adding a splash more water if needed to cook the veg. Add the noodles and half the soy sauce, and toss together. Divide between two bowls and keep warm.

2 Wipe out the wok and heat the remaining oil until smoking. Tip in the beef and stir-fry for 2 minutes over a high heat, but don't move it around too much initially or it will release liquid and stew rather than fry. Tip in the sesame seeds and the honey. Toss to coat the beef well, then add the remaining soy and bubble briefly. Spoon over the vegetables and noodles, and serve straight away.

· ·

PER SERVING 420 kcals, protein 32g, carbs 50g, fat 12g, sat fat 3g, fibre 8g, sugar 18g, salt 1.45g

Ham & ricotta pizzas with pesto

Ready-made pizza bases make a great speedy supper stand-by, but swap for white pitta bread if you'd like to make these more interesting.

 30 minutes 4

- 4 tbsp tomato pasta sauce
- 2 pizza bases
- 2 slices cooked ham, roughly torn
- ½ x 250g tub ricotta
- 1 tbsp fresh pesto

1 Heat oven to 220C/200C fan/gas 7. Put a baking sheet in the oven to heat up. Spread 2 tablespoons of the tomato sauce on each pizza base. Carefully slide the bases on to the baking sheet and cook them according to the pack instructions.

2 About 5 minutes before the cooking time is up, scatter over the ham, dot the ricotta on top in spoonfuls and continue cooking. Season and drizzle the pesto over each pizza before serving.

PER SERVING 282 kcals, protein 13g, carbs 43g, fat 7g, sat fat 3g, fibre 1g, sugar 4g, salt 1.51g

Vietnamese prawn salad

· ·

This no-cook supper makes great lunchbox food too – why not make double and save half for the next day?

 20 minutes 🥧 2 🌓 Easily doubled

FOR THE DRESSING
- 1 small garlic clove, finely chopped
- 1 small red chilli, deseeded and finely chopped
- 1 tbsp golden caster sugar
- juice 2 limes

FOR THE SALAD
- 250g/9oz thin rice noodles
- 150g pack cooked peeled tiger prawns, halved along their spines
- ½ cucumber, peeled, deseeded and cut into matchsticks
- 1 carrot, cut into matchsticks or grated
- 6 spring onions, shredded
- handful coriander and/or mint leaves
- 1 tbsp roasted peanuts, chopped

1 To make the dressing, mash together the garlic, chilli and sugar using a pestle and mortar. Add the lime juice and 3 tablespoons water, and stir together. Set aside.

2 Get the kettle on, put the noodles into a bowl, then cover with boiling water. Leave to stand for 10 minutes until tender, then drain and divide between two bowls.

3 Mix the prawns and veg together, and divide between the bowls. Finish by topping each salad with the herbs and peanuts, then pour over the dressing to serve.

· ·

PER SERVING 579 kcals, protein 27g, carbs 117g, fat 4g, sat fat 1g, fibre 2g, sugar 14g, salt 1.66g

Stir-fried Korean beef

· ·

Better and quicker to cook than anything you could phone up for, this impressive dinner for two is ideal for a Friday night in.

 20 minutes   2

- 1 tbsp soy sauce
- 1 tbsp mirin or clear honey
- 2 tsp cornflour, mixed to a paste with 2 tbsp water
- 1 tbsp vegetable oil
- 300g/10oz beef frying steak, thinly sliced
- 1 garlic clove, thinly sliced
- 1 red chilli, finely chopped
- 3 spring onions, sliced into small pieces
- 300g pack beansprouts
- 100g bag baby leaf spinach
- handful sesame seeds, toasted
- cooked rice, to serve (optional)

1 In a small bowl, mix together the soy, mirin or honey and cornflour paste. Heat the oil in a wok or large frying pan. Season the beef and sear in batches, then remove to a plate and cover with foil to keep warm. Fry the garlic and chilli, then add the spring onions and beansprouts, and stir-fry for 2 minutes until softened.

2 Return the beef to the wok and add the spinach along with the sauce. Keep stir-frying for another 2–3 minutes until the spinach has wilted and the sauce has coated the meat. Serve sprinkled with the sesame seeds and some rice, if you like.

· ·
PER SERVING 470 kcals, protein 40g, carbs 17g, fat 27g, sat fat 8g, fibre 6g, sugar 5g, salt 1.8g

Supersmoky bacon & tomato spaghetti

If your kids love the flavour of smoky chorizo sausage, you can replace the bacon with diced cooking chorizo and cook the sauce in exactly the same way.

🕐 25 minutes   🥧 4

- 400g/14oz spaghetti
- 1 tbsp olive oil
- 120g/4½oz smoked streaky bacon, sliced into matchsticks
- 1 onion, finely chopped
- 1 garlic clove, finely chopped
- 2 tsp sweet smoked paprika
- 2 x 400g cans chopped tomatoes
- grated Parmesan, to garnish (optional)

1 Bring a large pan of water to the boil and cook the spaghetti according to the pack instructions, then drain.

2 Meanwhile, heat the oil in a large non-stick frying pan and cook the bacon for 3–4 minutes until just starting to crisp. Stir in the onion and cook for another 3–4 minutes, then add the garlic and smoked paprika, and cook for 1 minute more. Pour in the chopped tomatoes, bring to the boil and bubble for about 5 minutes until thickened, stirring every so often to stop it catching on the bottom of the pan. Toss the drained pasta with the sauce and serve with Parmesan, if you like.

PER SERVING 500 kcals, protein 20g, carbs 80g, fat 12g, sat fat 3g, fibre 7g, sugar 11g, salt 1.2g

Refried bean quesadillas

For a more substantial meal, just double the amount of beans, roll up in 4 tortillas, sit in a baking dish, scatter with the salsa and cheese, and bake until piping hot.

🕐 30 minutes 🥧 4

- 1 tbsp sunflower oil
- 1 onion, finely chopped
- 2 garlic cloves, finely chopped
- 1 tsp cumin seeds
- 400g can pinto or kidney beans, drained and rinsed
- 2 tsp smoked paprika
- 8 flour tortillas
- 100g/4oz Cheddar or Gruyère, grated
- handful coriander leaves
- 200g/8oz pot fresh tomato salsa, plus extra to dip
- soured cream, for dipping

1 Heat the oil in a large frying pan, and cook the onion and garlic for 2 minutes. Add the cumin for 1 minute more. Tip in the beans, paprika and a splash of water. Using a potato masher, break the beans down as they warm through to make a rough purée. Season generously.

2 Spread the beans on to 4 of the tortillas and scatter over the cheese and coriander. Spoon the salsa over and top with remaining tortillas to make four sandwiches or quesadillas. Wipe the pan with kitchen paper and return to the heat or, alternatively, heat a griddle pan. Cook each sandwich for 1–2 minutes on each side until they are crisp and golden, and the cheese is melting. Serve warm, cut into wedges, with extra salsa and some soured cream for dipping.

PER SERVING 487 kcals, protein 20g, carbs 65g, fat 18g, sat fat 7g, fibre 7g, sugar 9g, salt 3.74g

BBQ chicken burgers

The easiest homemade burgers you'll ever make – you'll find most of the ingredients in your storecupboard or corner shop.

🕐 30 minutes   🍽 4

- 4 boneless skinless chicken breasts
- 4 rashers bacon
- 4 large burger buns, sliced in half
- lettuce, tomato and red onion, to serve

FOR THE SAUCE & MARINADE
- 4 tbsp tomato ketchup
- 4 tbsp brown sauce
- splash chilli sauce (optional)
- 2 tsp clear honey
- 2 garlic cloves, crushed

1 Make the sauce and marinade by mixing everything together in a large bowl, then set aside a few spoonfuls to use as sauce. Slice halfway into the thickest part of each chicken breast and open them up like a book. Flatten down slightly with your hand, then toss in the remaining marinade to coat.

2 Barbecue, griddle or fry the chicken in a non-stick frying pan for about 10 minutes until completely cooked through – turning it a few times so it doesn't burn but is nicely charred and sticky. Cook the bacon at the same time, until crisp, and toast the buns. Assemble the burgers with lettuce, slices of tomato, onion and the reserved sauce on the side for dolloping on top.

PER BURGER 406 kcals, protein 43g, carbs 48g, fat 6g, sat fat 2g, fibre 2g, sugar 8g, salt 1.96g

Steak with Mexican rice & beans

· ·

This dish is delicious just as it is, but if you'd like to up the veg count serve with a green salad dressed with a little lime juice.

 30 minutes   4

- 3 tbsp olive oil
- 1 large onion, sliced
- 200g/8oz long grain rice
- 2 tbsp fajita seasoning
- 400g can kidney beans, drained and rinsed
- 4 x 200g/8oz rump steaks
- small bunch coriander leaves, roughly chopped
- tomato salsa, to garnish

1 Heat 2 tablespoons of the oil in a medium pan and cook the onion for 3–4 minutes until golden. Stir in the rice and 2 teaspoons of the fajita seasoning, then cook for 1 minute. Pour in 600ml/1 pint boiling water and a pinch of salt, and stir. Cover and simmer for 15–20 minutes until all the water has been absorbed and the rice is tender. Stir in the beans and keep warm.

2 Meanwhile, rub the remaining oil, fajita seasoning and some salt and pepper over the rump steaks. Heat a griddle pan, then fry the steaks for 2–3 minutes on each side or until cooked to your liking. Stir the coriander into the rice and serve with the steaks, topped with a dollop of salsa.

· ·

PER SERVING 649 kcals, protein 48g, carbs 60g, fat 26g, sat fat 9g, fibre 5g, sugar 4g, salt 0.99g

Sweet potato, chickpea & chorizo hash

This supper can be adapted to suit your family – swap chorizo for bacon, sweet potatoes for normal spuds and chilli for a splash of brown sauce.

 30 minutes 4

- 600g/1lb 5oz sweet potatoes, diced
- 1 tbsp sunflower oil
- 1 large red onion, thinly sliced
- 400g/14oz cooking chorizo sausages, skinned and crumbled
- 400g can chickpeas, drained and rinsed
- 4 eggs
- 1 green chilli, thinly sliced into rings, to garnish

1 Boil the sweet potatoes for 8 minutes until tender, then drain. Meanwhile, heat the oil in a large ovenproof pan and cook the onion and chorizo for 5 minutes until softened. Add the sweet potatoes and chickpeas, and cook for 5 minutes more. Roughly break the mixture up with a fork, then flatten it down lightly to form a cake. Cook for a further 8 minutes, without stirring, until cooked through, crispy and golden on the bottom.

2 Heat grill to high. Break the eggs on to the hash, season, then put the pan under the grill and cook for 2–3 minutes until the whites are set. Sprinkle with chilli to serve.

PER SERVING 783 kcals, protein 34g, carbs 49g, fat 52g, sat fat 19g, fibre 8g, sugar 14g, salt 4.97g

Puff-pizza tart

This supper requires just four main ingredients and can be assembled in less than half an hour, without a knife or chopping board in sight.

🕐 25 minutes   🥧 4

- 375g sheet ready-rolled puff pastry
- 5 tbsp red pesto
- 70g pack sliced salami
- 125g ball mozzarella, torn into pieces
- drizzle extra virgin olive oil (optional)
- handful rocket leaves, to garnish (optional)

1 Heat oven to 220C/200C fan/gas 7. Unroll the pastry on to a large baking sheet and prick all over with a fork. Spread over the pesto, leaving a border of roughly 2.5cm/1in around the edge.

2 Layer on the salami, top with the torn mozzarella and some seasoning, then bake for 15–20 minutes until the pastry is golden, risen and crisp. Drizzle with a little oil and scatter over some rocket, if you like.

PER SERVING 597 kcals, protein 18g, carbs 28g, fat 47g, sat fat 19g, fibre 1g, sugar 1g, salt 2.29g

Homemade fish fingers

Much tastier than shop-bought and ready in only half an hour. Get the kids to help you coat the fish strips.

🕐 30 minutes   🥧 4

- 1 egg, beaten
- 85g/3oz white breadcrumbs, made from day-old bread
- zest and juice 1 lemon
- 1 tsp dried oregano
- 1 tbsp olive oil
- 400g/14oz skinless sustainable white fish, sliced into 12 strips
- 4 tbsp mayonnaise
- 100g/4oz baby leaf spinach
- 140g/5oz frozen peas, cooked and cooled

1 Heat oven to 200C/180C fan/gas 6. Pour the beaten egg into a shallow dish. Tip the breadcrumbs on to a plate. Mix the lemon zest into the breadcrumbs along with the oregano and some salt and pepper.

2 Brush a non-stick baking sheet with half the oil. Dip the fish strips into the egg, then roll them in the breadcrumbs. Transfer to the baking sheet and bake for 20 minutes until golden.

3 Meanwhile, mix the mayo with a squeeze of lemon juice. Toss the spinach leaves and peas with a squeeze more lemon juice and the remaining oil. Serve the fish fingers with the spinach and peas, with a spoonful of the lemony mayo on the side.

PER SERVING 336 kcals, protein 26g, carbs 21g, fat 17g, sat fat 3g, fibre 3g, sugar 2g, salt 0.88g

Full English kebabs

Everybody loves an all-day breakfast, and these clever kebabs combine the best elements of one.

🕐 20 minutes 🥧 4

- 1 tbsp olive oil
- 1 tbsp clear honey
- 1 tbsp wholegrain mustard
- 8 rashers streaky bacon, snipped in half
- 8 pork chipolatas, snipped in half
- 16 button or chestnut mushrooms
- 16 cherry tomatoes
- 4 small crusty baguettes or rolls
- salad leaves and tomato or brown sauce, to serve

1 Heat grill to high and mix together the oil, honey and mustard with a little seasoning, to taste, and set aside.

2 Wrap a piece of bacon around each half sausage, then start to load up the kebabs. On each skewer thread a mushroom, bacon-wrapped sausage chunk and a cherry tomato, then repeat so there are two of each ingredient on each skewer.

3 Brush the honey–mustard sauce over the skewers, then grill, turning, for 10 minutes until the sausages are golden, sticky and cooked through. Split the baguettes or rolls, and serve alongside the skewers with a handful of salad leaves and a dollop of tomato or brown sauce per person.

PER SERVING 282 kcals, protein 15g, carbs 7g, fat 21g, sat fat 7g, fibre 1g, sugar 5g, salt 2.05g

Quick chilli with creamy, crushed chive potatoes

. . . .

Using sausages instead of plain mince is a good way to add extra flavour to a dish. Look for varieties with flavourings like oregano, fennel or chilli.

🕐 25 minutes　🍕 4

- 454g pack reduced-fat pork sausages
- 2 tsp vegetable oil
- 1kg/2lb 2oz new potatoes, skins on, thickly sliced
- 2 red peppers, deseeded and sliced
- 2 garlic cloves, crushed
- 1 tsp each ground coriander, cumin and chilli powder
- 400g can red kidney beans in water, drained and rinsed
- 2 x 400g cans chopped tomatoes with herbs
- 2 tsp caster sugar
- 5 tbsp 0% fat Greek yogurt, plus extra to garnish (optional)
- 20g pack chives, snipped, plus extra to garnish (optional)

1 Squeeze three balls of meat from each sausage, then fry them in the oil for 5 minutes until golden. While they cook, put the potatoes on to boil for 10 minutes until tender. Add the peppers to the meatballs, then fry for 4 minutes more. Tip in the garlic and spices, fry for 1 minute, then add the beans, tomatoes and sugar. Simmer for 5 minutes until saucy and the meatballs are cooked.

2 Drain the potatoes, then crush with a masher. Fold through the yogurt and chives, loosen with a splash of water, then serve with the chilli. Top with a dollop more yogurt and an extra sprinkling of chives, if you like.

. . . .

PER SERVING 547 kcals, protein 31g, carbs 80g, fat 14g, sat fat 4g, fibre 11g, sugar 19g, salt 1.84g

Bacon, pea & basil macaroni

Adding vegetables to macaroni cheese is a good way of getting kids to eat more of them.

 30 minutes   4

- 6 rashers streaky bacon, chopped
- 2 leeks, finely sliced into rings
- 1 tbsp vegetable oil
- 140g/5oz frozen peas
- 400g/14oz macaroni
- 200g pack soft cheese
- 85g/3oz mature Cheddar, grated
- 1 tsp English mustard
- small bunch basil, shredded

1 Fry the bacon and leeks in an ovenproof frying pan in the oil for 10 minutes until the bacon is golden and the leeks soft. Tip in the peas and heat through. Meanwhile, cook the pasta according to the pack instructions and heat grill to high.

2 Reserve 150ml/¼ pint of the cooking water before you drain the pasta, then add the reserved water, the soft cheese, half the grated cheese and the mustard to the frying pan with the veg. Stir until the cheese melts into a creamy sauce. Stir in most of the basil and the pasta, then scatter with the rest of the grated cheese. Grill for 2–3 minutes until the cheese melts. Scatter with the remaining basil to serve.

PER SERVING 703 kcals, protein 28g, carbs 81g, fat 32g, sat fat 16g, fibre 6g, sugar 7g, salt 1.87g

Quick Caesar salad with roast chicken & bacon

．．．．．．．．．．．．．．．．．．．．．

Kids seem to love the tangy flavour of Caesar dressing, and this salad is easily turned into a burger if you're looking for something more substantial.

🕐 25 minutes   🥧 4

- 4 boneless chicken breasts, skin on
- 8 rashers streaky bacon
- 1 garlic clove, crushed
- juice ½ lemon
- 3 tbsp natural yogurt
- 3 tbsp olive oil
- 50g/2oz Parmesan, plus extra shavings to garnish (optional)
- dash Worcestershire sauce
- 2 small romaine lettuces

1 Heat oven to 200C/180C fan/gas 6. Season the chicken and put in a snug roasting tin. Drape the bacon around the chicken and roast for 15–20 minutes until the bacon is crisp and the chicken just cooked through.

2 In a bowl, mix the garlic, lemon juice, yogurt, oil and Parmesan, adding a dash of Worcestershire sauce. Discard the outer leaves of the lettuce and tear the rest over a platter, mixing them gently with the dressing. Serve the dressed leaves with the chicken and crisp bacon, shaving over extra Parmesan, if you like.

．．．．．．．．．．．．．．．．．．．．．．．

PER SERVING 480 kcals, protein 53g, carbs 2g, fat 29g, sat fat 10g, fibre none, sugar 2g, salt 1.65g

Tuna sweet-potato jackets

Colourful and full of fresh flavours, these jackets make a change to the usual bean-and-spud combo.

 30 minutes 4

- 4 sweet potatoes (about 200g/8oz each)
- 185g can tuna in spring water, drained
- ½ red onion, finely sliced
- 1 small red chilli, deseeded and chopped
- juice 1 lime
- 6 tbsp low-fat Greek yogurt
- handful coriander leaves, to garnish

1 Scrub the sweet potatoes and prick them all over with a fork. Put on a microwavable plate and cook on High for 18–20 minutes or until tender. Split in half and put each one, cut-side up, on a serving plate.

2 Flake the drained tuna with a fork and divide among the sweet potatoes. Top with the red onion and chilli, then squeeze over the lime juice. Top with a dollop of yogurt and scatter over the coriander to serve.

PER SERVING 238 kcals, protein 12g, carbs 44g, fat 3g, sat fat 2g, fibre 5g, sugar 13g, salt 0.32g

Nutty chicken curry

Unusual, but delicious; if you like peanuts you'll adore this easy curry-style dish. Leave out the extra chilli, if you don't think your kids will like it.

🕐 25 minutes   🍴 4

- 1 large red chilli, deseeded
- ½ finger-sized knob ginger, roughly chopped
- 1 garlic clove
- small bunch coriander, stalks roughly chopped
- 1 tbsp sunflower oil
- 4 boneless skinless chicken breasts, cut into chunks
- 5 tbsp peanut butter
- 150ml/¼ pint chicken stock
- 200g tub Greek yogurt
- boiled rice or mashed sweet potato, to serve

1 Finely slice and set aside a quarter of the chilli, then put the rest in a food processor with the ginger, garlic, coriander stalks and one-third of the leaves. Whizz to a rough paste with a splash of water, if needed.

2 Heat the oil in a frying pan, then quickly brown the chicken chunks for 1 minute. Stir in the paste for another minute, then add the peanut butter, stock and yogurt. When the sauce is gently bubbling, cook for 10 minutes until the chicken is just cooked through and the sauce is thickened (if it looks too thick, just add a splash of water). Stir in most of the remaining coriander, then scatter the rest on top with the reserved chilli. Eat with rice or mashed sweet potato.

Quick sausage stew

If your children aren't sure about the zesty topping, just serve it on the side and let everyone add their own.

 25 minutes 4

- 1 tbsp olive oil
- 12 pork chipolatas
- 1 onion, sliced
- 410g can chickpeas, drained and rinsed
- 350g jar ready-made tomato sauce
- 150ml/¼ pint chicken stock
- 1 garlic clove, finely chopped
- zest 1 small orange
- 2 tbsp chopped flat-leaf parsley
- crusty bread, to serve

1 Heat the oil in a deep frying pan and fry the sausages for 4–5 minutes until golden brown. Remove to a plate.

2 Cook the onion in the same pan until softened, about 5–6 minutes, adding a splash of water if it starts to catch. Add the chickpeas, tomato sauce and stock, and bring to the boil. Return the sausages to the pan, lower the heat to a simmer and cook for 5–6 minutes until the sausages are cooked through. Scatter the garlic, orange zest and parsley over the stew, then serve in shallow bowls with crusty bread on the side.

PER SERVING 373 kcals, protein 19g, carbs 23g, fat 24g, sat fat 6g, fibre 4g, sugar 9g, salt 2.48g

Cajun turkey wraps with sweetcorn salsa

· ·

These delicious wraps deserve a bowl of potato wedges on the side and a few leaves mixed with your favourite dressing.

🕐 20 minutes   🥧 4

- 1 tbsp Cajun spice mix
- 4 turkey breast steaks (about 500g/1lb 2oz total)
- 1 tbsp olive oil
- 330g can sweetcorn, drained and rinsed
- 1 red chilli, deseeded and finely chopped
- zest and juice ½ lime
- 8 flour tortillas
- 150ml pot soured cream (optional)
- salad leaves, to serve
- potato wedges and dressed salad, to serve

1 Sprinkle the spice mix evenly over the turkey. Heat the oil in a large pan, add the turkey and fry for 4 minutes on each side until cooked through. Rest for 2 minutes before thinly slicing.

2 Meanwhile, mix the sweetcorn with the chilli, lime zest and juice to make the salsa.

3 Warm the tortillas according to the pack instructions. To serve, assemble each wrap by spreading with a little soured cream, if liked, then pile on some sliced turkey and add a spoonful of salsa. Roll up and serve with some potato wedges and some dressed salad leaves.

· ·

PER SERVING 574 kcals, protein 42g, carbs 75g, fat 14g, sat fat 2g, fibre 4g, sugar 9g, salt 1.79g

Maple-glazed hot dogs with mustardy onions

· ·

Easily doubled if the kids have friends over, and you can also add French fries, baked beans and a big salad, if you're feeding a crowd.

🕐 30 minutes   🥧 4   🌓 Easily doubled

- 8 good-quality pork sausages
- 2 tbsp sunflower oil
- 2 onions, thinly sliced
- 1 tsp yellow or black mustard seeds
- 2 tbsp maple syrup
- 4 part-baked mini baguettes
- 1 tbsp Dijon mustard
- large pinch brown sugar
- 2 tsp wine vinegar or cider vinegar

1 Heat oven to 220C/200C fan/gas 7. Put the sausages on a non-stick baking sheet and roast for 15 minutes. Meanwhile, heat the oil in a frying pan and cook the onions and mustard seeds together for 10–15 minutes until softened and golden.

2 Remove the sausages from the oven and brush with maple syrup. Pop the baguettes on to the same baking sheet and cook the baguettes and sausages for 5–8 minutes until the sausages are dark, shiny and cooked through. Stir the mustard, sugar and vinegar into the onions until the sugar has melted. Cut the baguettes open across the top and put 2 sausages into each. Spoon over the mustardy onions and serve.

· ·

PER HOT DOG 498 kcals, protein 21g, carbs 43g, fat 28g, sat fat 8g, fibre 2g, sugar 12g, salt 2.37g

Spicy tuna pasta

If you don't want to cheat with a jar of sauce, add a 400g can chopped tomatoes, 1 tsp chilli flakes and 1 tsp sugar instead.

 25 minutes   4

- 2 x 185g cans tuna in spring water, drained
- 2 spring onions, chopped
- 1 egg, beaten
- 1 tbsp vegetable oil
- 350g jar tomato and chilli sauce
- 400g/14oz spaghetti
- ½ x 70g pack rocket leaves, roughly chopped

1 Squeeze the excess water from the tuna and put the fish in a bowl with the spring onions and egg, then stir together. Use your hands to shape the mixture into small walnut-sized balls – you should get about 12.
2 Heat the oil in a large non-stick frying pan, tip in the tuna balls, then cook for 5–10 minutes until golden all over. Pour over the tomato and chilli sauce, then cook for 5 minutes more, adding a little boiling water if the sauce looks dry.
3 Meanwhile, cook the pasta according to the pack instructions, then drain. Stir through the sauce along with most of the rocket. Serve in bowls with the remaining rocket on top.

PER SERVING 552 kcals, protein 33g, carbs 81g, fat 13g, sat fat 2g, fibre 4g, sugar 9g, salt 1.16g

Asian prawn & pineapple salad

Add rice or noodles to this vibrant salad if you need something more substantial, or just a handful of prawn crackers for something lighter.

 25 minutes 4

- 1 small pineapple or 350g/12oz pineapple chunks
- 140g/5oz beansprouts
- 250g/9oz cooked king prawns
- ½ cucumber, peeled, deseeded and sliced
- 200g/8oz cherry tomatoes, halved
- handful mint leaves, very roughly chopped, to garnish
- 50g/2oz unsalted cashew nuts, toasted, to scatter (optional)

FOR THE DRESSING

- ½ red chilli, deseeded and sliced
- 1 garlic clove
- 1 tsp golden caster sugar
- juice 2 limes
- 1½ tsp fish sauce

1 Mash the chilli, garlic and sugar for the dressing to a paste using a pestle and mortar or small food processor. Stir in the lime juice and fish sauce.

2 If using fresh pineapple, peel, quarter, core and slice the fruit at an angle into chunks. Toss the pineapple chunks with the beansprouts, prawns, cucumber, tomatoes and some of the dressing. Pile into bowls and scatter with the mint and cashews, if using. Drizzle with the rest of the dressing and serve.

PER SERVING 202 kcals, protein 19g, carbs 17g, fat 7g, sat fat 1g, fibre 3g, sugar 14g, salt 1.5g

Two bean, potato & tuna salad

You'll find soya beans in the vegetable section of the supermarket freezer cabinet.
If you can't find them, just use frozen broad beans.

 25 minutes 4

- 300g/10oz new potatoes, cut into chunks
- 175g/6oz green beans, trimmed and halved
- 175g/6oz frozen soya beans
- 160g can tuna in water, drained well
- good handful rocket or watercress leaves, to garnish

FOR THE DRESSING
- 2 tsp harissa paste
- 1 tbsp red wine vinegar
- 2 tbsp olive oil

1 Put the potatoes in a pan of boiling water, then boil for 6–8 minutes until almost tender. Add both types of beans, then boil for a further 5 minutes until everything is cooked. Meanwhile, make the dressing. Whisk together the harissa and vinegar with a little seasoning. Whisk in the oil. Drain the potatoes and veg well, toss with half the dressing, then leave to cool.

2 Flake the tuna, then fold into the potatoes. Add the remaining dressing then gently toss. Divide among four bowls and serve each portion with a handful of rocket or watercress on top. Serve warm or cold.

PER SERVING 211 kcals, protein 15g, carbs 19g, fat 9g, sat fat 1g, fibre 4g, sugar 2g, salt 0.14g

Turkey burgers with beetroot relish

These burgers freeze really well, so why not make double and have dinner ready in the freezer for another night?

 25 minutes 4

- 500g pack minced turkey
- ½ tsp dried thyme or 2 tsp fresh
- 1 lemon
- Little Gem lettuce and wholemeal pitta breads, to serve

FOR THE RELISH
- 250g/9oz cooked peeled beetroot (not in vinegar), finely diced
- 1 small red onion, finely chopped
- 2 tbsp chopped parsley
- 2 tsp olive oil
- 2 tsp wholegrain mustard

1 Tip the turkey into a bowl with the thyme. Finely grate in the zest from the lemon and add a little seasoning. Use your hands to mix the ingredients well, then shape into four patties. Chill until ready to cook. (Can be frozen for up to 1 month.)

2 Mix the beetroot for the relish with the juice from half the zested lemon, the onion, parsley, oil and mustard. Grill, griddle or barbecue the burgers for about 6 minutes on each side and serve with the beetroot relish, lettuce and pitta breads.

PER SERVING 183 kcals, protein 30g, carbs 7g, fat 4g, sat fat 1g, fibre 2g, sugar 6g, salt 0.5g

Zesty rice-noodle salad

Thin rice noodles need no cooking – simply soaking in boiling water is enough to soften them.

 30 minutes 4

- 250g/9oz vermicelli rice noodles
- 4 carrots, cut into matchsticks
- 1 large red onion, thinly sliced
- handful each mint and coriander leaves
- juice 6 limes
- 2 tbsp caster sugar
- 1 tbsp fish sauce
- 2 red chillies, cut into thin slices
- drizzle vegetable oil
- 300g/10oz lean minced pork

1 Pour boiling water over the noodles and let them sit for 5 minutes. Rinse them under cold water and drain before putting in a serving bowl. Add the carrots, onion and half the herbs.

2 Meanwhile, make the dressing by mixing the lime juice, sugar and fish sauce along with half the chillies.

3 Heat a non-stick frying pan or wok until extremely hot, then add the oil. Cook the mince until it browns, breaking it up with the back of a wooden spoon and making sure it is cooked through. Tip over the noodle mixture, then toss over the dressing, giving everything a good mix. Serve with the remaining herbs and chilli slices scattered on top.

PER SERVING 392 kcals, protein 25g, carbs 67g, fat 4g, sat fat 2g, fibre 3g, sugar 18g, salt 0.94g

Summer salad with anchovy dressing

Anchovies are strong in flavour, so remember that a little goes a long way – if you don't like them, add a splash of Worcestershire sauce instead.

🕐 25 minutes 🥧 4

- 140g/5oz green beans
- 300g/10oz new potatoes, sliced
- 4 eggs
- handful pitted black olives
- 200g/8oz cherry tomatoes, halved
- 2 Baby Gem lettuces, leaves separated

FOR THE DRESSING
- 2 anchovy fillets in oil
- 1 tbsp red wine vinegar
- 3 tbsp olive oil

1 Bring a large pan of water to the boil. Cook the beans for 4 minutes, so they still have a slight crunch, then scoop out with a slotted spoon into a colander and cool quickly with cold water. Tip the potatoes into the pan of boiling water, add the eggs and simmer everything for 8 minutes. Lift out the eggs, then leave to cool while the potatoes cook for 2 more minutes until tender. Drain the potatoes.

2 For the dressing, mash the anchovies with the side of a knife, then mix with the vinegar and oil in a large bowl. Stir in the beans, potatoes, olives and tomatoes. Peel and halve the eggs. Put the leaves into a large serving bowl, add the potato mix and eggs, then serve.

PER SERVING 256 kcals, protein 11g, carbs 15g, fat 17g, sat fat 3g, fibre 3g, sugar 4g, salt 0.54g

One-pan chicken couscous

. . . .

Satisfying yet superhealthy. Any leftovers will make a delicious lunch the next day – add a small handful of sultanas with the apricots, if you like.

🕐 15 minutes 🥘 4

- 1 tbsp olive oil
- 1 onion, thinly sliced
- 200g/8oz boneless skinless chicken breasts, diced
- thumb-sized knob ginger
- 1–2 tbsp harissa paste, plus extra to serve (optional)
- 10 dried apricots
- ½ x 400g can chickpeas, drained and rinsed
- 200g/8oz couscous
- 200ml/7fl oz hot chicken stock
- handful coriander, chopped, to garnish

1 Heat the oil in a large frying pan and cook the onion for 1–2 minutes just until softened. Add the chicken and fry for 7–10 minutes until cooked through and the onions have turned golden. Grate over the ginger then stir through the harissa to coat everything and cook for 1 minute more.

2 Tip in the apricots, chickpeas and couscous, then pour over the stock and stir once. Cover with a lid or tightly cover the pan with foil and leave for about 5 minutes until the couscous has soaked up all the stock and is soft. Fluff up the couscous with a fork and scatter over the coriander to serve. Serve with extra harissa, if you like.

. . . .

PER SERVING 281 kcals, protein 20g, carbs 41g, fat 6g, sat fat 1g, fibre 3g, sugar 9g, salt 0.48g

Spiced mackerel with parsley & orange salad

· ·

An orange salad works brilliantly with mackerel as the citrus tang makes a nice, fresh contrast to the oiliness of the fish.

🕐 30 minutes   🍽 2

- 2 fresh mackerel (about 200g/8oz each), gutted and heads removed
- ½ tsp paprika
- ¼ tsp each ground cumin and coriander
- 2 tsp olive oil

FOR THE SALAD
- 3 small oranges
- small bunch flat-leaf parsley, roughly chopped
- 1 small red onion, finely chopped
- drizzle extra virgin olive oil

1 Heat grill to high. Cut three fairly deep slashes through the skin and into the flesh on either side of the fish with a sharp knife. Mix the spices into a paste with the oil, then rub it over the fish, especially into the slashes. Put on a baking sheet and grill for 12 minutes, turning the fish over halfway through so that both sides cook evenly.

2 Meanwhile, make the salad. Cut the peel and pith from the oranges with a sharp knife and cut the oranges into slices. Put them in a bowl and toss with the parsley and red onion.

3 Serve the mackerel with the salad, drizzled with a little extra virgin olive oil.

· ·

PER SERVING 449 kcals, protein 31g, carbs 20g, fat 28g, sat fat 5g, fibre 4g, sugar none, salt 0.27g

Kedgeree with poached egg

Kedgeree is traditionally served as a breakfast dish, but it also makes a great hearty weekend brunch – or try this quick, healthy version for a weeknight dinner.

🕐 30 minutes 🥧 4

- 300g/10oz long grain rice
- 2 tbsp olive oil
- 1 onion, finely chopped
- 2 garlic cloves, finely chopped
- 390g pack fish pie mix, defrosted if frozen
- 1 heaped tbsp mild or medium curry powder
- juice 1 lemon
- ¼ small pack parsley, chopped
- 4 eggs

1 Cook the rice according to the pack instructions, then drain and set aside.
2 Meanwhile, heat 1 tablespoon of the oil in a non-stick frying pan and cook the onion and garlic for 5 minutes. Toss the fish pieces with the curry powder and the remaining oil. Add to the pan. Cook for another 5 minutes, stirring carefully and turning the fish.
3 Add the rice to the pan and turn up the heat, then stir well (the fish will break up a little). Cook for 1–2 minutes, then stir in the lemon and parsley. Turn the heat down as low as it will go, and cover with a lid.
4 Bring a pan of water to the boil, turn down the heat and poach the eggs. Season the kedgeree and divide among bowls, topping each with a poached egg.

PER SERVING 542 kcals, protein 31g, carbs 63g, fat 17g, sat fat 4g, fibre 3g, sugar 2g, salt 0.7g

Spanish rice & prawn one-pot

This easy one-pot can be on your table in under half an hour. Add a little smoked paprika, if you have any.

🕐 25 minutes   🥧 4

- 1 onion, sliced
- 1 red and 1 green pepper, deseeded and sliced
- 50g/2oz chorizo, sliced
- 2 garlic cloves, crushed
- 1 tbsp olive oil
- 250g/9oz easy-cook basmati rice
- 400g can chopped tomatoes
- 200g/8oz raw peeled prawns, defrosted if frozen

1 Boil the kettle. In a non-stick frying or shallow pan with a lid, fry the onion, peppers, chorizo and garlic in the oil over a high heat for a few minutes until the veg is beginning to soften. Stir in the rice and chopped tomatoes with 500ml/18fl oz boiling water, cover, then cook over a high heat for 12 minutes.

2 Uncover, then stir – the rice should be almost tender. Stir in the prawns, with a splash more water if the rice is looking dry, then cook for another minute until the prawns are just pink and the rice is tender.

PER SERVING 356 kcals, protein 19g, carbs 59g, fat 7g, sat fat 2g, fibre 4g, sugar 7g, salt 0.85g

Cajun chicken & chunky bean salsa

The seasoning and salsa here also work well with salmon fillets – just grill them for 5 minutes instead.

🕐 30 minutes   🥧 2

- 2 boneless skinless chicken breasts
- ½ tsp olive oil
- 1 tbsp Cajun seasoning

FOR THE SALSA
- 400g can pinto beans, drained and rinsed
- 2 red peppers, deseeded and diced
- 1 avocado, diced
- 2 spring onions, sliced
- 1 tbsp olive oil
- juice 1 lemon
- handful coriander leaves, chopped

1 To make the salsa, tip the beans, peppers, avocado and spring onions into a bowl. Season, dress with the oil and lemon juice, and set aside.

2 Lay the chicken breasts on a board and bash a bit to flatten them out slightly. Put the flattened chicken in a dish, drizzle with the oil, then coat with the Cajun seasoning. Heat a griddle or frying pan and cook the chicken for 5 minutes on each side, until cooked all the way through. Stir the coriander through the salsa just before serving with the chicken.

PER SERVING 579 kcals, protein 48g, carbs 45g, fat 24g, sat fat 3g, fibre 16g, sugar 11g, salt 0.4g

Moroccan mushrooms with couscous

· ·

This vegetarian supper provides three of your 5-a-day. For an extra crunch, stir some pumpkin or sunflower seeds into the couscous.

🕐 30 minutes   🥧 4

- 1 red onion, sliced
- 1 tsp olive oil
- ½ tsp ground cinnamon
- 1 tsp ground cumin
- 300g/10oz mushrooms, quartered
- 400g can chopped tomatoes
- 410g can chickpeas, drained and rinsed
- 1 tsp clear honey
- 175g/6oz couscous
- 50g/2oz soft dried apricots, diced
- handful flat-leaf parsley, roughly chopped
- green beans, to serve

1 Fry the onion in the oil for 6 minutes until softened. Add the cinnamon and cumin, and cook for 1 minute, stirring. Add the mushrooms, cook for 2 minutes, then stir in the tomatoes, chickpeas and honey. Season and simmer for 7–8 minutes.

2 Meanwhile, mix the couscous with the dried apricots and some seasoning in a bowl. Pour over 250ml/9fl oz boiling water, stir to mix, then cover. Leave to stand for 7 minutes or until softened.

3 To serve, fluff up the couscous with a fork, stir in the parsley and top with the mushroom mixture. Great served with green beans.

· ·

PER SERVING 245 kcals, protein 11g, carbs 44g, fat 4g, sat fat none, fibre 6g, sugar 11g, salt 0.51g

Poached fish with ginger & sesame broth

. . . .

Low-fat, healthy, packed with flavour and really quick to make – what more do you want from a weeknight supper?

🕐 20 minutes ⏲ 2

- 500ml/18fl oz fish stock
- 1 tbsp rice wine vinegar
- 2 slices ginger
- 2 garlic cloves, shredded
- 85g/3oz frozen soya beans or peas
- 100g/4oz Tenderstem broccoli, halved if large
- 4 Chinese leaves or 1 small pak choi, sliced
- 3 spring onions, sliced at an angle
- 2 chunky skinless white fish fillets, such as haddock or sustainable cod
- few drops sesame oil
- ½–1 tsp toasted sesame seeds

1 Pour the stock into a deep sauté pan or wok with the vinegar, then add the ginger and garlic. Cover and cook for 5 minutes to allow the flavours to mingle.

2 Add the soya beans or peas, broccoli and the fleshy part of the Chinese leaves or pak choi, then put the spring onions and fish on top. Cover and cook for 4–5 minutes more until the fish just flakes. Carefully lift the fish off on to a plate, discard the ginger, and stir in the remaining Chinese leaf or pak choi and the sesame oil. Ladle the veg and stock into bowls, top with the fish and sprinkle with the seeds.

. . . .
PER SERVING 247 kcals, protein 40g, carbs 6g, fat 6g, sat fat 1g, fibre 5g, sugar 1g, salt 0.7g

Fruity pork steaks

· ·

A delicious winter warmer that's good for you too. Apples can be swapped for pears, and redcurrant jelly for a caramelised onion relish.

 30 minutes 4

- 4 boneless pork loin steaks, fat trimmed
- 2 tsp Chinese five-spice powder
- 1 tbsp sunflower oil
- 1 large red onion, cut into thin wedges through the root
- 4 red apples, cored and each cut into 8
- 2 tbsp redcurrant jelly
- 1 tbsp red wine vinegar or cider vinegar
- 200ml/7fl oz chicken stock

1 Dust the pork steaks with the Chinese five-spice powder. Heat half the oil in a frying pan and fry the pork for about 3 minutes on each side until browned and cooked through. Transfer to a plate.

2 Add the remaining oil to the frying pan, then fry the onion wedges for 2 minutes. Add the apples and cook, stirring occasionally, for another 3 minutes. Add the redcurrant jelly to the pan, followed by the vinegar and then the stock. Bring to the boil and simmer rapidly, uncovered, for 8–10 minutes until the sauce is slightly syrupy and the apples are tender. Gently reheat the pork in the sauce, turning to glaze each side.

· ·

PER SERVING 304 kcals, protein 33g, carbs 25g, fat 9g, sat fat 2g, fibre 3g, sugar 24g, salt 0.79g

Oriental cod & vegetables

· ·

Light but lovely – the perfect simple steamed dish that cooks while you get on with something else.

 25 minutes 2

- 85g/3oz baby corn, halved lengthways
- 85g/3oz shiitake mushrooms, halved
- 2 x 140g/5oz skinless cod fillets
- 2 tsp dark soy sauce
- 1 tbsp rice wine
- 1 tbsp clear honey
- 1 garlic clove, thinly sliced
- ½ red chilli, thinly sliced
- ½ finger-sized knob ginger, cut into matchsticks
- 2 pak choi heads, halved
- steamed rice, to serve

1 Line the base and sides of a steamer with a large sheet of baking parchment. Add the corn and mushrooms in an even layer, then sit the cod on top. Mix the soy, rice wine and honey with the garlic, chilli and ginger, then spoon half over the fish. Lay the pak choi over the cod and drizzle with the remaining soy mixture.

2 Add water to the base of the steamer, cover tightly and steam for 10–15 minutes or until the cod flakes easily. Serve the cod and veg with its juices and some steamed rice.

· ·
PER SERVING 187 kcals, protein 30g, carbs 13g, fat 2g, sat fat none, fibre 2g, sugar 11g, salt 1.4g

Chicken, kale & sprout stir fry

To make this recipe gluten-free, check that your noodles are made from 100 per cent buckwheat or use rice noodles, and swap the soy sauce for tamari.

🕐 30 minutes   🥧 2

- 100g/4oz soba noodles
- 100g/4oz shredded curly kale
- 2 tsp sesame oil
- 2 lean boneless, skinless chicken breasts, sliced into thin strips
- 25g/1oz piece ginger, peeled and cut into matchsticks
- 1 red pepper, deseeded and thinly sliced
- handful Brussels sprouts, cut into quarters
- 1 tbsp low-sodium soy sauce
- 2 tbsp rice wine vinegar or white wine vinegar
- zest and juice 1 lime

1 Cook the noodles according to the pack instructions, then drain and set aside.

2 Meanwhile, heat a large wok or frying pan, add the kale along with a good splash of water and cook for 1–2 minutes until wilted. Transfer to a colander and cool under running water to keep the colour of the leaves.

3 Add half the oil to the wok or pan and cook the chicken strips until browned, then remove to a plate. Heat the remaining oil and fry the ginger, pepper and sprouts until softened a little. Return the chicken and kale to the wok or pan and add the noodles. Tip in the soy, rice wine or white wine vinegar and lime zest and juice along with enough water to create a sauce that clings to the ingredients. Serve immediately.

PER SERVING 381 kcals, protein 36g, carbs 50g, fat 6g, sat fat 1g, fibre 5g, sugar 7g, salt 2.1g

Broccoli & sage pasta

Sage adds a lovely savoury note to this delicious pasta dish. If you have any fresh chillies left over from another dish, then swap them for the crushed version here.

🕐 20 minutes   🥧 2

- 140g/5oz quick-cook spaghetti
- 140g/5oz Tenderstem broccoli, trimmed and cut into 5cm/2in lengths
- 3 tbsp olive oil
- 2 shallots, sliced
- 1 garlic clove, finely chopped
- ¼ tsp crushed chillies
- 12 sage leaves, shredded
- grated Parmesan, to garnish (optional)

1 Bring a pan of water to the boil and cook the spaghetti for 1 minute. Add the broccoli and cook for 4 minutes more.

2 Meanwhile, heat the oil in a frying pan and add the shallots and garlic. Gently cook for 5 minutes until golden. Add the chillies and sage to the pan and gently cook for 2 minutes. Drain the pasta and broccoli, mix with the shallot mixture in the pan, then scatter with Parmesan, if you like.

PER SERVING 419 kcals, protein 12g, carbs 55g, fat 19g, sat fat 3g, fibre 5g, sugar 4g, salt 0.03g

Herbed goat's-cheese & summer-veg tarts

. . . .

These tarts can be prepared up to a day before and kept covered in the fridge ready to be cooked – just give them 5 minutes more from cold.

🕐 30 minutes   🍽 4

- 320g pack ready-rolled puff pastry
- a little plain flour, for dusting
- 150g tub soft goat's cheese
- 1 tsp herbes de Provence, or chopped herbs from the garden
- 2 small courgettes, cut into thin rounds
- 5 tomatoes (not too big), thinly sliced
- handful pitted black olives
- leaves from a few thyme sprigs
- drizzle extra virgin olive oil
- medium egg, beaten, to glaze

FOR THE SALAD
- 1 tbsp mild olive oil
- 2 tsp red wine vinegar
- 1 tsp Dijon mustard
- 1 tsp clear honey
- 100g bag watercress leaves

1 Heat oven to 220C/200C fan/gas 7. Unroll the pastry and cut it into four rectangles. Score a border about 2cm/¾in from the edge of each piece, then lift on to a lightly floured baking sheet. Mash the goat's cheese with the herbs, plus some seasoning. Spread over the middles of the tarts.

2 Overlap the courgette and tomato slices on top of the cheese, then scatter with the olives and thyme leaves. Drizzle with a little olive oil. Brush the edges of the pastry with the beaten egg. Bake for 15–20 minutes until the pastry is dark golden and the vegetables are starting to sizzle.

3 Whisk together the oil, vinegar, mustard and honey to make a dressing, then season to taste. Toss with the watercress just before serving the dressed leaves on top of the tarts.

. . . .

PER SERVING 515 kcals, protein 16g, carbs 34g, fat 35g, sat fat 17g, fibre 2g, sugar 6g, salt 1.5g

Coconut noodle & vegetable soup

Swap the green curry paste for red or yellow – just choose whichever flavour and brand is your favourite.

 25 minutes   4

- 1–2 tbsp Thai green curry paste
- 1 tsp groundnut oil
- 700ml/1¼ pints vegetable stock
- 300ml/½ pint reduced-fat coconut milk
- 200g/8oz thick rice noodles
- 200g/8oz chestnut mushrooms, sliced
- 140g/5oz sugar snap peas, halved
- 100g/4oz beansprouts
- 1½ tbsp fish sauce
- juice 1 lime
- 3 spring onions, shredded, few mint and coriander leaves, to garnish

1 Put a large pan over a medium heat. Cook the curry paste in the oil for 1 minute until it starts to release its aroma. Pour in the stock and coconut milk, and bring to the boil. Reduce the heat to a simmer and stir in the noodles. Simmer for 7 minutes, then stir in the mushrooms and sugar snaps. Cook for 3 minutes more, then add the beansprouts, fish sauce and lime juice. Remove the pan from the heat.

2 Ladle the noodles and soup into bowls, then scatter with spring onions, mint and coriander to serve.

PER SERVING 296 kcals, protein 7g, carbs 48g, fat 10g, sat fat 7g, fibre 3g, sugar 5g, salt 1.97g

Courgette & lemon linguine

This dish is made all in one pan with only seven ingredients in just 20 minutes. Grating courgettes is a clever way to avoid having to cook them first.

🕐 20 minutes   🥧 4

- 400g/14oz linguine
- 3 courgettes, coarsely grated
- 3 tbsp olive oil, plus extra to drizzle (optional)
- 1 garlic clove, finely chopped
- zest 1 lemon
- large pinch crushed chillies
- handful basil leaves, torn

1 Cook the linguine according to the pack instructions, then drain quickly so some cooking water is still clinging to the strands. Tip back into the cooking pan with the grated courgettes, oil, garlic, lemon zest, chillies and most of the basil. Season generously, then use tongs to toss everything together.
2 Scatter with the remaining basil leaves and add an extra drizzle of oil to serve, if you like.

PER SERVING 435 kcals, protein 15g, carbs 76g, fat 10g, sat fat 2g, fibre 4g, sugar 5g, salt 0.26g

Halloumi with broccoli tabbouleh & honey-harissa dressing

Stir a spoonful of any leftover harissa through a tub of houmous for a delicious North-African-inspired dip that works well in a grown-up lunchbox.

🕐 15 minutes   🍽 4

- 140g/5oz couscous
- 300g/10oz broccoli florets
- 6 spring onions, finely sliced
- 150g/5oz cherry tomatoes, quartered
- large bunch parsley, finely chopped
- small bunch mint, finely chopped
- juice 2 lemons, zest ½ lemon
- 2½ tbsp extra virgin olive oil
- 1½ tbsp harissa paste
- 1 tbsp clear honey
- 2 x 250g packs halloumi, cut into 1cm-/½in-thick slices
- 25g/1oz toasted flaked almonds

1 Put the couscous into a bowl and cover with boiling water. Cover with cling film and set aside for 5 minutes.

2 Cook the broccoli for 2 minutes in a pan of boiling water, then drain well. Cut into small pieces or blitz in a food processor.

3 Fork the broccoli, spring onions, tomatoes, herbs, lemon zest, the juice of 1½ lemons and 2 tablespoons of the oil through the couscous. Season and mix well.

4 To make the dressing, combine the harissa, honey, remaining lemon juice and oil and some seasoning.

5 Heat a non-stick frying pan and cook the halloumi for 1–2 minutes on each side until golden. Pile the couscous on to a serving platter, top with the halloumi slices and dressing, then scatter over the almonds.

PER SERVING 682 kcals, protein 36g, carbs 32g, fat 44g, sat fat 22g, fibre 5g, sugar 8g, salt 4g

Bean, chickpea & feta salad

Even if there are only two to feed, make the full quantity of this salad and save the leftovers for lunch the next day.

 15 minutes 4

- 400g/14oz green beans, trimmed and halved
- 3 tbsp olive oil
- 2 x 400g can chickpeas, drained and rinsed
- 1 garlic clove, roughly chopped
- 7 sun-dried tomatoes in oil, drained
- 2 whole roasted red peppers from a jar
- 1 tbsp sherry vinegar
- 200g pack feta, broken into chunks

1 Heat oven to 200C/180C fan/gas 6. Spread the beans on to a baking sheet, season, and drizzle over 1 tablespoon of the oil. Roast for 10 minutes until lightly charred. Tip into a bowl along with the chickpeas.

2 In a food processor, make a dressing by whizzing together the garlic, sun-dried tomatoes, peppers, vinegar and the remaining oil. Season, stir into the beans with the feta and serve.

PER SERVING 404 kcals, protein 20g, carbs 28g, fat 25g, sat fat 8g, fibre 10g, sugar 6g, salt 2.92g

Japanese tofu-noodle bowl

Straight-to-wok noodles are brilliant time-savers when you need food in a flash. You'll find them next to the dried variety in your local supermarket.

 30 minutes ⊙ 4

- 3 tbsp dark soy sauce
- 2 tbsp seasoned rice vinegar
- 1 tbsp mirin or 2 tsp caster sugar
- 200g/8oz firm tofu, drained, patted dry and cut into 8 cubes
- cornflour, for coating
- sunflower oil, for frying
- 1 bunch asparagus, trimmed and each spear cut into about 4 pieces
- 50g/2oz fresh or frozen edamame beans
- 50g/2oz frozen peas
- ½ thumb-sized knob of ginger, grated
- 400g pack straight-to-wok udon noodles
- coriander leaves, to garnish
- chilli oil, to drizzle

1 Combine the soy sauce, vinegar and mirin or sugar in a bowl, stirring until dissolved. Add the tofu and turn to coat.

2 Turn oven on low to warm. Scatter the cornflour over a plate. Remove the tofu from the marinade, reserving the liquid, and roll in cornflour to coat all sides. Heat a frying pan with enough sunflower oil to cover the base. Fry the tofu, turning occasionally, until golden and crisp all over. Drain on kitchen paper, then keep warm in the oven.

3 Put 1 litre/1¾ pints water in a pan with the reserved marinade and bring to the boil. Add the vegetables and ginger, and simmer until the veg are almost tender, about 2–3 minutes, then add the noodles for another minute. Ladle among four bowls and divide the tofu on top. Top with coriander leaves and drizzle with a little chilli oil.

PER SERVING 478 kcals, protein 20g, carbs 87g, fat 8g, sat fat 1g, fibre 3g, sugar 6g, salt 5.02g

Lentil & lemon fettuccine

This simple peasant-style dish is hugely satisfying and packed with protein, plus it's unusual and interesting enough to entertain with.

 25 minutes 4

- 300g/10oz fettuccine or linguine
- 50g/2oz butter
- 1 medium onion, chopped
- 3 garlic cloves, chopped
- 400g can puy or brown lentils, drained and rinsed
- zest and juice 1 lemon
- large handful coriander, leaves and stems roughly chopped
- 150g tub low-fat Greek yogurt

1 Cook the pasta according to the pack instructions or until al dente.
2 Meanwhile, melt the butter in a frying pan over a medium heat and add the onion. Cook until softened, then add the garlic for 2 minutes. Stir in the lentils to heat through.
3 Drain the pasta and return it to the pan. Stir in the lentil mixture with the lemon zest and juice, coriander and yogurt and some seasoning.

PER SERVING 511 kcals, protein 21g, carbs 76g, fat 16g, sat fat 9g, fibre 6g, sugar 6g, salt 0.28g

Spicy tofu kedgeree

Keep vegetarian food interesting with this tasty supper for two, and if you like it less spicy use a mild curry powder instead.

🕐 30 minutes   🥧 2

- 140g/5oz basmati rice
- 2 eggs
- 1 tbsp olive oil
- 1 onion, chopped
- 1 red chilli, deseeded and chopped (leave seeds in, if you like it spicy)
- 2 tbsp medium curry powder
- 1 tsp brown or black mustard seeds
- 2–3 pinches cayenne pepper
- 100g/4oz marinated tofu, cubed
- ½ bunch spring onions, sliced
- handful flat-leaf parsley, chopped

1 Cook the rice and boil the eggs in the same pan of boiling water for 8–9 minutes. Meanwhile, heat the oil in a non-stick frying pan and soften the onion and chilli for 5 minutes. Add all the spices and fry for 1–2 minutes more.

2 Drain the rice and stir into the spicy onion with a splash of water and the tofu. Season well, then heat through gently for a few minutes until piping hot. Peel and quarter the boiled eggs. Stir the spring onions and parsley into the rice, divide between two bowls and top with the eggs.

PER SERVING 574 kcals, protein 25g, carbs 68g, fat 25g, sat fat 4g, fibre 6g, sugar 5g, salt 2.3g

Mushroom & chickpea burgers

Veggie burgers can sometimes be bland and boring, but these taste really substantial and are packed with flavour.

🕐 30 minutes 🍽 4

- 1 tbsp olive oil
- 250g/9oz chestnut mushrooms, finely chopped
- 2 garlic cloves, crushed
- 1 bunch spring onions, sliced
- 1 tbsp medium curry powder
- zest and juice ½ lemon
- 400g can chickpeas, drained and rinsed
- 85g/3oz fresh wholemeal breadcrumbs
- 6 tbsp 0% fat Greek yogurt
- pinch ground cumin
- 2 mixed-grain muffins or rolls, toasted and halved
- 2 plum tomatoes, sliced
- handful rocket leaves

1 Heat 1 teaspoon of the oil in a non-stick frying pan and cook the mushrooms, garlic and spring onions for 5 minutes. Mix in the curry powder, lemon zest and juice, and cook for about 2 minutes or until the mixture looks quite dry. Tip out on to a plate to cool slightly.

2 Use a potato masher or fork to mash the chickpeas in a bowl, leaving a few chunky pieces. Add the mushroom mix and the crumbs, then shape into four patties. Fry in the remaining oil for 3–4 minutes on each side until crisp and browned.

3 Mix the yogurt with the cumin. Put half a muffin or roll on each plate, then spread with the cumin yogurt. Top with the burgers, a few slices of tomato and a little rocket.

· ·

PER SERVING 271 kcals, protein 15g, carbs 40g, fat 7g, sat fat 1g, fibre 6g, sugar 4g, salt 1.13g

Tortellini & pesto minestrone

One of the quickest dinners you'll ever make. Swap the flavour of tortellini according to your mood.

 10 minutes 4

- 1.5 litres/2¾ pints strong vegetable stock
- 500g pack spinach and ricotta tortellini
- 500g/1lb 2oz spring greens, washed and finely shredded
- 140g/5oz peas (frozen or fresh)
- 4 tbsp pesto

1 Bring the stock to the boil in a large pan. Tip in the pasta and cook according to the pack instructions, throwing in the spring greens and peas with 1–2 minutes to go.

2 When the vegetables are tender, pasta is cooked and the broth is piping hot, stir through the pesto and spoon into bowls. Top with a good grind of black pepper and serve

PER SERVING 493 kcals, protein 21g, carbs 73g, fat 15g, sat fat 6g, fibre 10g, sugar 11g, salt 2.63g

Falafel tabbouleh with lemon yogurt

Look for different-flavoured falafels in the supermarket to add variety to this dish. Sweet-potato ones work nicely.

 25 minutes 4

- 16 ready-made falafels
- 200g/8oz couscous
- 2 large lemons, 1 zested, juice of both
- 3 tbsp olive oil
- 1 bunch spring onions, finely sliced
- 1 cucumber, halved and sliced
- small bunch mint, leaves roughly chopped
- large bunch parsley, leaves roughly chopped
- 150g tub natural yogurt

1 Cook the falafels according to the pack instructions and boil the kettle. Tip the couscous into a large bowl, pour over 300ml/½ pint boiling water, cover, then leave to stand for 5 minutes until all of the water is absorbed.
2 Fluff up the couscous with a fork, then stir through the lemon zest, juice from 1½ lemons, oil, spring onions, cucumber, mint and three-quarters of the parsley with plenty of seasoning. Tip on to a large platter.
3 Mix the remaining lemon juice and parsley into the yogurt, then spoon into a small bowl. Scatter the hot falafels over the tabbouleh, then serve the lemon yogurt alongside.

PER SERVING 478 kcals, protein 14g, carbs 53g, fat 25g, sat fat 4g, fibre 8g, sugar 12g, salt 1.36g

Roasted aubergine, tomato & basil pasta

. . . .

This summertime pasta is simple, but packed with Mediterranean flavours. Roast chunks of courgettes in with the aubergine, if you have any.

🕐 20 minutes   📊 2

- 1 large aubergine, cut into chunks
- 2 tbsp olive oil
- 2 fat garlic cloves, unpeeled
- 300g pack cherry tomatoes
- 1 tbsp balsamic vinegar
- 1 tsp caster sugar
- 250g/9oz pasta, such as penne or fusilli
- handful basil leaves, plus extra to garnish

1 Heat oven to 220C/200C fan/gas 7. Toss the aubergine chunks with the oil and whole garlic cloves into a roasting tin with some seasoning. Roast for 10 minutes, add the tomatoes, vinegar and sugar, then cook for another 5 minutes. Meanwhile, cook the pasta according to the pack instructions, then drain.

2 When the veg is tender, remove the garlic cloves, snip off their ends and squeeze the roasted garlic on to a board. Mash with a fork, then stir this garlic paste back into the veg with the basil leaves – squashing most of the tomatoes as you go. Tip in the cooked pasta, stir everything together in the roasting tin, divide between two bowls, then scatter with a few more basil leaves to serve.

. . . .

PER SERVING 610 kcals, protein 18g, carbs 108g, fat 15g, sat fat 2g, fibre 9g, sugar 15g, salt 0.1g

Goat's cheese, pea & bean frittata

The perfect standby supper! You can use whatever cheese you have in the fridge – goat's cheese, Brie or soft cheese all work well.

 25 minutes 4

- 300g/10oz mix frozen peas and beans
- 8 eggs
- splash milk
- 100g log goat's cheese (the kind with rind)
- 1–2 tbsp chopped mint leaves

1 Heat grill to medium. Boil the peas and beans for 4 minutes until just tender, then drain well. Beat the eggs with a splash of milk and some seasoning. Slice four thin, round slices of goat's cheese (you'll use about half the log) and reserve. Roughly chop or crumble the rest of the cheese into pieces, then stir this into the eggs with the veg and mint.

2 Heat an ovenproof shallow pan, pour in the egg mix and gently cook over a low heat for 8–10 minutes until there is just a little un-set mix on the surface. Top with the slices of goat's cheese, then grill until set, golden and the cheese is bubbling.

PER SERVING 306 kcals, protein 25g, carbs 8g, fat 20g, sat fat 7g, fibre 4g, sugar 2g, salt 0.74g

Cauliflower & cashew pilaf with chickpea curry

• •

This pilaf is perfect served with any curry you like. Make a chicken version for meateaters and a chickpea one for vegetarians.

🕐 30 minutes   🍽 4

- 2 tbsp vegetable oil
- 1 onion, chopped
- 100g/4oz cashew nuts
- 200g/8oz basmati rice
- 400g/14oz cauliflower, cut into small florets
- 425g jar curry sauce (try dopiaza)
- 400g can chickpeas, drained and rinsed
- handful coriander leaves, roughly chopped, to garnish

1 Heat the oil in a large pan, add the onion and fry until lightly coloured. Add the cashews and fry until golden. Stir in the rice until coated in the oil. Add the cauliflower and 600ml/1 pint water, season, then bring to the boil. Cover, then gently cook for 12–15 minutes until the rice and cauliflower are tender.

2 Meanwhile, heat the curry sauce and chickpeas together, then simmer for 5 minutes. Spoon the rice into four shallow bowls and spoon the curry on the side. Scatter over the coriander and serve.

• •
PER SERVING 608 kcals, protein 18g, carbs 71g, fat 29g, sat fat 5g, fibre 8g, sugar 13g, salt 1.65g

Walnut & red-pepper pesto pasta

It's well worth making your own pesto – this one, with sweet red peppers and earthy walnuts, knocks spots off shop-bought jars.

 30 minutes 4

- 400g/14oz strozzapreti or casarecce pasta, or another short pasta shape
- 100g/4oz walnuts
- 3 roasted red peppers, roughly chopped
- 25g/1oz Parmesan or vegetarian alternative, grated, plus extra to garnish
- 1 small garlic clove, roughly chopped
- large pack fresh basil, plus a few leaves to garnish
- 2 tbsp extra virgin olive oil
- 50g/2oz mascarpone

1 Cook the pasta according to the pack instructions.
2 Meanwhile, toast the walnuts in a dry pan for a few minutes. Add half the walnuts to the small bowl of a food processor or a hand chopper, along with the red peppers, Parmesan or veggie alternative, garlic, basil, oil and some seasoning. Whizz to a paste, adding a splash of water from the pasta if it is a little dry.
3 Drain the pasta, reserving a cup of the cooking water. Return the pasta to the pan and set over a low heat. Add the pesto, mascarpone and 3–4 tablespoons of the reserved pasta water, then stir until the mascarpone has melted, adding a splash more pasta water if the sauce needs thinning.
4 To serve, crush the remaining walnuts in your hand and scatter over the pasta with a few more basil leaves and some extra Parmesan or veggie alternative.

PER SERVING 589 kcals, protein 19g, carbs 56g, fat 33g, sat fat 8g, fibre 1g, sugar 2g, salt 0.2g

Quick steak grill

· ·

Who needs to head out for dinner when this steak supper for two is ready in a flash?
Swap the watercress for some peas, if you prefer.

 25 minutes   2

- 1 large unpeeled potato
- 3 tbsp olive oil
- 2 large flat-cap mushrooms, stalks removed
- 2 tomatoes
- 2 sirloin steaks (about 140g/5oz each)
- ¼ beef stock cube
- large handful watercress

1 Heat grill to high. Thickly slice the potato then lay the slices on a large non-stick baking sheet and brush with some of the oil. Grill for 10 minutes until browned. Flip over the potatoes, add the mushrooms and tomatoes to the sheet and brush with a little more oil, then return everything to the grill for another 10 minutes until cooked.

2 Heat the remaining oil in a frying pan. Season the steaks, then sear for 1½–2 minutes on each side, depending how you like your steak cooked. Remove and leave to rest. Add a splash of water to the pan, crumble in the stock cube, then boil to make a thin gravy, adding any steak juices from the plate. Serve the steaks with the veg, a handful of watercress and the gravy.

· ·

PER SERVING 510 kcals, protein 34g, carbs 23g, fat 32g, sat fat 9g, fibre 4g, sugar 4g, salt 0.72g

Salmon with sesame, soy & ginger noodles

This recipe proves that entertaining isn't always about cooking for a crowd–sometimes you just want to share a smart dinner with a friend.

🕐 30 minutes   🥧 2

- 4 tbsp soy sauce
- 4 tbsp rice wine
- 1 ball stem ginger, finely chopped, plus 2 tbsp syrup from the jar
- 1 garlic clove, crushed
- 2 salmon fillets
- 140g/5oz any noodles
- 2 tbsp sesame seeds
- 2 spring onions, chopped

1 Heat oven to 180C/160C fan/gas 4. In a small jug, whisk together the soy, rice wine, stem ginger and syrup and garlic. Line a roasting tin with baking parchment and put the salmon in it. Pour over half the sauce, then bake for 15 minutes until the salmon is cooked through.

2 Meanwhile, bring a large pan of water to the boil. Add the noodles and cook according to the pack instructions, then drain well.

3 In a small frying pan, lightly toast the sesame seeds for 1 minute (reserving a sprinkle for the top), then add to the cooked noodles. Pour the remaining sauce over the noodles, plus any left in the roasting tin, and toss. Serve with the salmon, scattered with the chopped spring onions and reserved sesame seeds.

PER SERVING 749 kcals, protein 42g, carbs 78g, fat 27g, sat fat 5g, fibre 4g, sugar 27g, salt 4g

Creamy crab & pea pasta

Fresh crab is a real treat, and its delicate flavour means it needs very little cooking – just tossing the crabmeat through fresh pasta is enough to heat it through.

 15 minutes 4

- 400g/14oz spaghetti
- 200g/8oz fresh or frozen peas
- 300g/10oz fresh crabmeat
- 5 tbsp reduced-fat crème fraîche
- 1 red chilli, deseeded and chopped
- handful parsley leaves, chopped
- zest 1 lemon, juice ½ lemon

1 Boil a large pan of salted water, tip in the pasta, then cook for about 7 minutes. Add the peas, then cook for 2–3 minutes more until both are cooked through.

2 Drain in a colander, reserving a little cooking water, then tip the pasta and peas back into the pan with the crabmeat and crème fraîche. Stir well with the remaining ingredients, reserving a little chilli, parsley and lemon zest to garnish. Add some pasta cooking water if the mixture seems dry. Serve sprinkled with the remaining chopped chilli, parsley and lemon zest.

PER SERVING 512 kcals, protein 31g, carbs 81g, fat 10g, sat fat 3g, fibre 5g, sugar 5g, salt 0.83g

Buttery trout with capers

· ·

Only five ingredients are needed in this simple but special supper. Just add green beans or a salad and some boiled new potatoes to complete the meal.

 15 minutes 4

- 4 thick trout fillets
- 100g/4oz butter
- squeeze lemon juice
- handful parsley, leaves chopped
- 2 tbsp capers, rinsed
- green beans or salad and boiled new potatoes, to serve

1 Heat oven to 200C/180C fan/gas 6. Rinse the fish, then pat dry with kitchen paper. Put in a roasting tin, season, then dot with a third of the butter. Roast for 10–12 minutes.

2 When the fish is almost ready, melt the remaining butter in a frying pan. Turn up the heat until the butter turns brown. Take off the heat and add the lemon juice, parsley and capers. Pour over the fish, then serve.

· ·

PER SERVING 345 kcals, protein 28g, carbs 1g, fat 26g, sat fat 14g, fibre none, sugar none, salt 1.04g

Mozzarella & salami ciabatta

This no-cook creation makes a great starter for eight, or a superb summery light supper or lunch for four.

 10 minutes 4 or 8

- 2 small ciabatta, cut in half
- 2 small fennel bulbs, trimmed and thinly sliced
- 2 tbsp extra virgin olive oil
- 2 handfuls rocket leaves
- 2 garlic cloves, halved
- 125g ball mozzarella (use a light version if you prefer), drained
- 16 slices salami
- lemon wedges, to garnish

1 Slice each ciabatta half into two, lengthways, and toast on one side. Meanwhile, toss the fennel with 2 teaspoons of the oil, the rocket and some seasoning.

2 Rub the remaining oil on the toasted sides of the bread, then rub with the cut sides of the garlic. Tear over the mozzarella and add the salami slices, pile on the salad and serve with some lemon wedges for squeezing over.

PER SERVING (4) 519 kcals, protein 23g, carbs 47g, fat 28g, sat fat 10g, fibre 4g, sugar 4g, salt 2.99g

Hot-smoked salmon salad with chilli–lemon dressing

· ·

Thrown together in minutes, yet stylish enough for entertaining, this dish is a great one to have up your sleeve.

🕐 30 minutes   🍴 8

- 500g/1lb 2oz new potatoes, halved
- 200g pack asparagus tips
- 250g bag mixed salad leaves
- small bunch each parsley and mint, leaves picked and roughly chopped
- 140g/5oz radishes, thinly sliced
- 8 hot-smoked salmon steaks, skin removed
- 4 spring onions, sliced

FOR THE DRESSING
- 3 tbsp lemon juice
- 125ml/4fl oz olive oil
- 1 tsp wholegrain mustard
- 2 red chillies, deseeded and finely chopped

1 Boil the potatoes in a pan of salted water for 10 minutes until tender, adding the asparagus tips for the final 2 minutes of cooking. Drain and allow to cool a little while you get the remaining ingredients ready. Whisk together the dressing ingredients, then season to taste.

2 In a large bowl, toss together the potatoes, asparagus, salad leaves, herbs and radishes. Add two-thirds of the dressing, thoroughly mix through the salad, then spread the salad over a large platter. Break the hot-smoked salmon into large chunks, then scatter over the top with the spring onions. Pour the remaining dressing over the top.

· ·

PER SERVING 299 kcals, protein 21g, carbs 13g, fat 19g, sat fat 3g, fibre 2g, sugar 3g, salt 2.09g

Creamy linguine with prawns

Ready in a flash for a romantic night in, or easily doubled to serve to friends who drop by unexpectedly.

 20 minutes　🍳 2　◑ Easily doubled

- 175g/6oz linguine
- 2 tsp olive oil
- 1 garlic clove, finely sliced
- 100ml/3½fl oz white wine
- 2 tbsp reduced-fat crème fraîche
- juice ½ lemon (or to taste)
- 2 handfuls (about 140g/5oz total) raw peeled prawns
- small bunch chives, finely snipped

1 Cook the pasta according to the pack instructions. Meanwhile, heat the oil in a pan and gently fry the garlic for 2 minutes. Tip in the wine and bubble over a high heat for 1 minute, then lower the heat and stir in the crème fraîche and lemon juice. Season to taste with salt and plenty of black pepper. Simmer for 1 minute to reduce a little, then add the prawns and simmer in the sauce until just pink.

2 Drain the pasta and tip into the sauce with half the chives. Use tongs to mix everything together. Divide between two shallow bowls and sprinkle with the remaining chives.

PER SERVING 441 kcals, protein 25g, carbs 67g, fat 8g, sat fat 2g, fibre 2g, sugar 6g, salt 0.62g

Steak salad with blue-cheese vinaigrette

. . . .

This salad is special enough for entertaining – just add some freshly toasted bread, rubbed with a garlic clove and drizzled with olive oil.

🕐 25 minutes   🥧 2

- 1 fillet or rump steak (about 300g/10oz total), trimmed
- 140g/5oz green beans, trimmed
- 1 chicory head, leaves separated
- 25g/1oz walnuts, roughly chopped

FOR THE DRESSING

- zest and juice ½ lemon
- 1 tbsp walnut or olive oil
- 1 tbsp tarragon leaves, chopped
- 1 small shallot, finely chopped
- 2 tbsp blue cheese, crumbled

1 Season the steak with lots of black pepper and a little salt. Cook on the barbecue or under a really hot grill for 2–3 minutes each side, or to your liking. Leave to rest for 10 minutes, then slice.

2 Meanwhile, cook the beans in a pan of boiling water until just tender. Drain and rinse under cold water, then drain very thoroughly.

3 For the dressing, whisk together the lemon zest and juice, oil, tarragon, shallot, cheese and some seasoning.

4 Divide the chicory leaves between two plates and top with the beans, walnuts and steak slices. Pour the dressing over the salad just before you are ready to serve.

. . . .
PER SERVING 402 kcals, protein 40g, carbs 5g, fat 25g, sat fat 7g, fibre 3g, sugar 3g, salt 0.7g

Pan-fried trout with bacon, almonds & beetroot

. . . .

Three fillets fit snugly into the average-sized frying pan, but if cooking for four the warm-salad part to this recipe will easily stretch, if you need it to.

🕐 30 minutes   🥧 3

- 1 tbsp olive oil
- 25g/1oz butter
- 3 trout fillets, pin-boned
- 200g/8oz bacon lardons
- ¼ loaf (about 140g/5oz) sourdough bread, cut into croutons
- handful flaked almonds
- 85g bag watercress leaves
- 250g/9oz beetroot (not in vinegar), cut into small chunks

FOR THE DRESSING
- 3 tbsp olive oil
- 1 tbsp red wine vinegar

1 Heat 1 teaspoon of the olive oil with the butter in a large non-stick frying pan until it just starts to sizzle. Add the fish, skin-side down, and fry for 10–15 minutes – basting often until the skin is crisp and the flesh has cooked through – then turn over for a minute. Remove and keep warm.

2 Add the remaining oil to the pan and tip in the bacon lardons and croutons. Fry for about 10 minutes until crisp. Meanwhile, toast the flaked almonds in a dry pan over a medium heat.

3 In a small bowl, whisk together the oil and vinegar for the dressing with some seasoning.

4 Toss the watercress, beetroot, lardons, croutons, almonds and dressing together in a large bowl. Sit a trout fillet on each plate and serve with the salad on the side.

. . . .
PER SERVING 729 kcals, protein 47g, carbs 33g, fat 45g, sat fat 13g, fibre 4g, sugar 9g, salt 2.9g

Creamy spiced mussels

Mussels are good value and quick to cook but seem special enough for entertaining. Serving with a bowl of chips will make this dish more substantial.

 30 minutes 4

- 2 shallots, finely chopped
- 25g/1oz butter
- 1 tsp plain flour
- 1–2 tsp curry paste
- 150ml/¼ pint dry white wine
- 2kg/4lb 8oz fresh mussels, scrubbed and any open ones discarded
- 100g/4oz crème fraîche
- chopped parsley, to garnish
- crusty bread or chips, to serve

1 Fry the shallots in the butter in a large pan until they are softened, but not browned. Stir in the flour and curry paste, and cook for 1 minute.

2 Stir in the wine, tip in the mussels, then cover and cook for 3–4 minutes, shaking the pan occasionally until the mussels open. Tip everything into a colander set over a large bowl to catch the juices. Discard any mussels that haven't opened.

3 Return the juices to the pan with the crème fraîche and bubble for a minute. Divide the mussels among four bowls, spoon over the sauce, scatter with parsley and eat with crusty bread or chips.

PER SERVING 285 kcals, protein 19g, carbs 6g, fat 18g, sat fat 10g, fibre 1g, sugar none, salt 1.27g

Thai shredded chicken & runner-bean salad

. . . .

Thai basil has a more aniseed flavour than ordinary basil, but if you can't find any, use coriander instead.

🕐 30 minutes 🥧 4

- 200g/8oz runner beans
- 1 red chilli, halved, deseeded and finely sliced
- 2 shallots, finely sliced
- 1 lemongrass stalk, finely sliced
- ½ thumb-sized knob ginger, shredded
- 2 cooked boneless skinless chicken breasts, shredded
- small bunch mint
- large bunch Thai basil
- 1 lime, cut in wedges, to garnish
- jasmine rice, to serve

FOR THE COCONUT DRESSING
- 100ml/3½fl oz coconut cream
- 1 garlic clove, crushed
- 3 tbsp fish sauce
- 1 tsp sugar
- juice 1 lime
- 1 red chilli, deseeded and finely diced

1 Top and tail the runner beans, peel off the stringy bits and slice. Cook the beans in a pan of simmering salted water for 4 minutes or until tender but still bright green. Drain and put in a bowl with the chilli, shallots, lemongrass, ginger and chicken.

2 Mix all the dressing ingredients together. Tear the mint and Thai basil over the chicken and toss everything together. Pile on to a plate and pour over the dressing. Serve with the lime wedges to squeeze over and some jasmine rice.

. . . .

PER SERVING 214 kcals, protein 23g, carbs 6g, fat 11g, sat fat 8g, fibre 1g, sugar 5g, salt 2.31g

Hot-smoked salmon, lentil & pomegranate salad

. . . .

The unusual combination of these flavours will wow your guests. Serve with some toasted pitta on the side for an added crunch.

🕐 30 minutes   🥧 4

- 4 tbsp extra virgin olive oil
- juice 1 lemon
- 2 garlic cloves, finely chopped
- 4 tbsp roughly chopped tarragon leaves
- 2 tsp clear honey
- 2 small red onions or 1 large, thinly sliced
- 2 x 400g can Puy lentils, drained and rinsed
- 300g/10oz hot-smoked salmon
- large bunch flat-leaf parsley, leaves picked
- 2 pomegranates, seeds removed
- toasted pitta bread, to serve

1 Combine the oil, lemon juice, garlic, tarragon and honey in a large bowl and season. Toss in the red onion and lentils, and set aside to marinate for 10 minutes.
2 Break the salmon into large flakes and fold into the salad with the parsley and pomegranates. Serve with toasted pitta.

. . . .

PER SERVING 382 kcals, protein 27g, carbs 31g, fat 18g, sat fat 3g, fibre 11g, sugar 13g, salt 3.19g

Grilled mackerel with orange, chilli & watercress salad

• •

Light, yet packed with flavour. Serve this salad with rice cooked with a couple of cardamom pods and a small cinnamon stick.

🕐 30 minutes   🥧 4

- 1 tsp black peppercorns
- 1 tsp coriander seeds
- 4 oranges
- 1 red chilli, deseeded, finely chopped
- 8 fresh mackerel fillets
- 1 tsp wholegrain mustard
- 1 tbsp clear honey
- 120g bag watercress, spinach and rocket salad
- 1 shallot, thinly sliced

1 Finely crush the peppercorns and coriander seeds with a pestle and mortar. Mix with the grated zest from half an orange and half the chopped chilli. Lightly slash the skin of the mackerel and press the zesty, peppery mixture on to the fish. Heat grill to high.

2 Segment the oranges. Slice the top and bottom off each orange, then cut away the peel and any white pith using a small, sharp knife. Holding each orange over a bowl to catch the juices, cut down either side of each segment to release it, then squeeze the shells to release any extra juice. Measure 4 tablespoons of this juice into a small bowl and mix with the mustard, honey and remaining chilli.

3 Grill the mackerel, skin-side up, for 4 minutes or until cooked through. Meanwhile, divide the salad leaves among plates and scatter with orange segments and shallot. Drizzle with dressing and top with mackerel.

• •

PER SERVING 412 kcals, protein 30g, carbs 18g, fat 25g, sat fat 5g, fibre 3g, sugar 17g, salt 0.32g

Peppered steak–tortilla salad

If you want to make this salad more special, crumble a little blue cheese over before serving.

 20 minutes  4

- 2 soft flour tortillas
- 2 tbsp olive oil
- 4 small thin-cut sirloin steaks, trimmed of any fat (about 85g/3oz each)
- 2 ripe avocados
- 4 tbsp mustard mayonnaise
- 120g bag watercress, rocket and spinach salad

1 Heat oven to 200C/180C fan/gas 6. Brush each tortilla with a little of the oil, then bake on a baking sheet in the oven for 6–8 minutes until crisp.

2 Meanwhile, rub a little more of the oil over the steaks and generously season. Heat a griddle or frying pan until hot, then cook the steaks for 1–2 minutes each side, depending on the thickness of your steak and how you like it cooked. Remove from the pan and rest on a plate while you prepare the other ingredients.

3 Stone and peel the avocados, then thickly slice. Whisk the mustard mayo with the remaining oil, 2 teaspoons water and the resting juices from the steaks to make a dressing. Break the tortillas into pieces and slice the steak, trimming off any more excess fat. Divide the salad among four plates, top with the avocado, tortilla pieces, sliced steak and finally drizzle with the dressing.

PER SERVING 453 kcals, protein 22g, carbs 16g, fat 34g, sat fat 6g, fibre 3g, sugar 2g, salt 0.64g

Vietnamese caramel trout

A caramel base is a cornerstone for savoury Vietnamese cooking – it balances out the other hot and salty ingredients and creates a deeply flavoured sauce.

 20 minutes 2

- 50g/2oz golden caster sugar
- 1 tbsp Thai fish sauce
- 1 red chilli, finely sliced
- large knob ginger, peeled and finely sliced
- 2 rainbow trout fillets, skin on
- 2 heads pak choi, halved
- juice ½ lemon
- a few coriander leaves, to garnish
- steamed rice, to serve

1 Put the sugar in a large shallow pan with a lid along with a small splash of water. Heat gently, swirling the pan, until the sugar has dissolved. Increase the heat and bubble the syrup until it turns a dark amber colour. Add the fish sauce, most of the chilli and ginger, then splash in 1 tablespoon water to dilute. Boil again until syrupy, then add the fish fillets, skin-side down, and the pak choi, cut-side down.

2 Cover the pan with the lid and simmer for 4–5 minutes until the fish is cooked and the pak choi has wilted. Turn off the heat, squeeze over the lemon and scatter with the remaining chilli and ginger and the coriander leaves. Serve with steamed rice.

PER SERVING 301 kcals, protein 31g, carbs 28g, fat 8g, sat fat 2g, fibre 2g, sugar 27g, salt 1.9g

Watermelon, prawn & avocado salad

This superhealthy dish makes a great light lunch or starter – perfect in the summertime when the weather is warm and melon is in season.

 15 minutes   4

- 1 small red onion, finely chopped
- 1 fat garlic clove, crushed
- 1 small red chilli, deseeded and finely chopped
- juice 1 lime
- 1 tbsp rice or white wine vinegar
- 1 tsp caster sugar
- watermelon wedge, deseeded and diced
- 1 avocado, diced
- small bunch coriander leaves, chopped
- 200g pack cooked tiger prawns, defrosted if frozen

1 Put the onion in a medium bowl with the garlic, chilli, lime juice, vinegar, sugar and some seasoning. Leave to marinate for 10 minutes.
2 Add the watermelon, avocado, coriander and prawns, then toss gently to serve.

PER SERVING 179 kcals, protein 13g, carbs 14g, fat 8g, sat fat 1g, fibre 2g, sugar 13g, salt 0.91g

Creamy sausage & rocket linguine

Choose good-quality sausages with a high pork content for this filling and super-fast Italian-inspired dish.

🕐 20 minutes   🥧 4

- 8 pork sausages
- 2 tsp olive oil
- 400g/14oz linguine
- 100g/4oz rocket leaves
- 1–2 red chillies, seeds in or out (depending on how hot you like it), finely chopped
- 150ml/¼ pint single cream

1 Squeeze the sausage meat out of the skins, breaking it into grape-sized chunks. Heat the oil in a frying pan. Fry the chunks for about 8 minutes until crisp and golden.

2 Meanwhile, cook the pasta according to the pack instructions and chop most of the rocket. Add the chillies to the sausages, fry for 30 seconds, then tip in the cream and chopped rocket. Season and heat until the rocket has just wilted.

3 Drain the pasta, reserving some of the cooking liquid, then mix the pasta through the sauce with a splash of cooking water. Top with the remaining rocket leaves.

PER SERVING 825 kcals, protein 29g, carbs 81g, fat 45g, sat fat 19g, fibre 3g, sugar 6g, salt 1.72g

Salmon with warm chickpea, pepper & spinach salad

Swap the chickpeas for any pulses you like – Puy lentils, butter beans or cooked barley all work well.

🕐 20 minutes   🍽 2

- 1 large red pepper, quartered and deseeded
- zest and juice ½ small lemon
- pinch smoked paprika (try sweet smoked)
- 1 tbsp extra virgin olive oil
- 100g/4oz baby leaf spinach
- 2 x 140g/5oz skinless salmon fillets
- 400g can chickpeas

1 Heat the grill to high. Squash the pepper quarters flat and grill for 5 minutes or until well blackened. Leave the grill on, then transfer the peppers to a bowl, cover with cling film and leave to cool slightly before peeling off the skins and cutting the flesh into strips. Set aside.

2 Make the dressing by whisking together the lemon zest and juice, paprika, oil and some seasoning. Toss half the dressing with the spinach leaves and divide between two dishes.

3 Season the salmon and grill for 5 minutes or until just cooked through. Meanwhile, heat the chickpeas in their canning liquid in a pan for 3–4 minutes. Drain well, then mix with the remaining dressing and the strips of pepper. Spoon the chickpea mix over the spinach and top with the salmon to serve.

PER SERVING 481 kcals, protein 39g, carbs 26g, fat 25g, sat fat 4g, fibre 7g, sugar 7g, salt 1.02g

Gooseberry & elderflower mess

Adding only half the sugar at the start of the recipe means that you can adjust it to taste later, depending on the sharpness of the gooseberries you're using.

🕐 30 minutes   🥧 6

- 300g/10oz gooseberries (we used red ones), tops pinched off
- 50g/2oz golden caster sugar, plus extra 2 tbsp
- 2 tbsp elderflower cordial
- 600ml pot whipping cream
- about 100g/4oz meringues (4–5 large nests), roughly crumbled

1 Put the gooseberries, 2 tablespoons water and 25g/1oz of the sugar in a small pan. Gently cook until the gooseberries are just softening and breaking down. Taste, adding more of the remaining 25g/1oz sugar as you need, then set aside to cool.

2 Put the extra 2 tablespoons sugar, the cordial and cream in a big bowl and whisk until soft peaks form, then cover and chill until ready to serve.

3 Just before serving, swirl the gooseberry compote, cream and crumbled meringues together, and spoon into six serving glasses or bowls.

PER SERVING 505 kcals, protein 3g, carbs 32g, fat 41g, sat fat 25g, fibre 2g, sugar 33g, salt 0.1g

Quick sticky-toffee puddings

Dressing up shop-bought muffins makes this pudding a doddle. If you can get toffee or caramel ones it'll be even more delicious!

 15 minutes   4

- 4 large chocolate muffins, crumbled
- 50g/2oz large sultanas
- small knob butter, for greasing
- vanilla ice cream, to serve

FOR THE SAUCE
- 50g/2oz light muscovado sugar
- 50g/2oz butter
- 75ml/2½fl oz double cream

1 Heat oven to 200C/180C fan/gas 6. Mix the muffins with the sultanas. Divide among four buttered ramekins or put in one baking dish. Cover with foil and bake for 8 minutes until just warmed through.

2 Meanwhile, put the sugar, butter and cream for the sauce in a small pan and gently heat together, stirring until the sugar dissolves. Pour the sauce over the muffin mixture and serve warm with ice cream.

PER SERVING 555 kcals, protein 5g, carbs 59g, fat 35g, sat fat 20g, fibre 1g, sugar 42g, salt 0.66g

Spiced-glazed pineapple with cinnamon fromage frais

· ·

This low-fat pud is perfect any time of the year and works as a light but tasty finish to any curry.

🕐 20 minutes   🥧 4

- zest and juice 1 lime
- 2 tbsp clear honey
- 2 pinches ground cinnamon
- few gratings whole nutmeg
- 2 tsp icing sugar, sifted
- 200g/8oz very low-fat fromage frais
- 2 tsp butter
- 1 fresh pineapple, cut into 8 long wedges, skin and core removed

1 Mix the lime juice and half the zest with half the honey, a pinch of the cinnamon and the nutmeg. Set this sauce aside. Stir the icing sugar and a further pinch of cinnamon into the fromage frais.

2 Heat the butter and remaining honey in a non-stick frying pan until melted. Add the pineapple and cook over a high heat for 8 minutes, turning regularly until caramelised. Pour in the spiced lime sauce and bubble for a few seconds, tossing the pineapple to glaze in the sauce. Serve immediately, sprinkled with the remaining lime zest and accompanied by a dollop of the cinnamon fromage frais.

· ·

PER SERVING 159 kcals, protein 5g, carbs 31g, fat 3g, sat fat 1g, fibre 2g, sugar 30g, salt 0.1g

Microwave banana pudding

A microwave makes very short work of a sponge pudding – perfect for weeknights when you suddenly fancy something sweet.

 20 minutes   4

- 100g/4oz butter, softened, plus extra for greasing
- 2 ripe bananas
- 100g/4oz light muscovado sugar
- 100g/4oz self-raising flour
- 2 tsp ground cinnamon
- 2 eggs
- 2 tbsp milk
- icing sugar, to dust
- toffee sauce, to drizzle
- ice cream, to serve (optional)

1 Put the butter in a 1-litre baking dish and microwave on High for 30 seconds –1 minute until melted. Add 1½ of the bananas, mash into the melted butter, then add the sugar, flour, cinnamon, eggs and milk. Mix together well.

2 Slice the remaining banana over the top, then return to the microwave and cook on High for 8 minutes until cooked through and risen. Serve warm, dusted with icing sugar with a drizzle of toffee sauce and a scoop of ice cream, if you like.

PER SERVING 474 kcals, protein 7g, carbs 57g, fat 26g, sat fat 15g, fibre 1g, sugar 37g, salt 0.77g

Mango & passion-fruit fool

. . . .

This fruity fool can be made ahead so dessert is even easier. Use fat-free yogurt to make it healthier.

🕐 10 minutes, plus chilling   🥧 4

- 2 large ripe mangoes
- 4 passion fruit, halved
- juice 1 lime
- 2 x 150g tubs low-fat Greek yogurt

1 Peel the mangoes using a vegetable peeler. Slice the cheeks off one and cut into dice.
2 Cut the flesh from the remaining mango and stone, then purée the flesh in a liquidiser. Squeeze out the seeds from two of the passion-fruit halves and mix with the mango purée. Add lime juice to taste. Gently fold the yogurt and half the diced mango through the fruity purée.
3 Divide among four glasses and top with the remaining diced mango. Chill until ready to eat. Scoop the seeds from the remaining passion fruit over the top of the fools to serve.

. . . .
PER FOOL 390 kcals, protein 3g, carbs 27g, fat 30g, sat fat 19g, fibre 5g, sugar 27g, salt 0.06g

Berry-crumble pots

This pud is great for using up any biscuits or fruit you might have to hand. Try ginger biscuits with sliced banana, for example.

 10 minutes ⏲ 4

- 2 tbsp good-quality strawberry jam
- juice 2 clementines or satsumas
- 300g/10oz mixed berries
- 150ml/¼ pint custard
- 4 tbsp double cream, lightly whipped
- 8 amaretti biscuits

1 Mix the jam and citrus juice together in a bowl. Stir in the berries. Divide half the jammy berries among four glasses or small bowls. Top with the custard, the rest of the berries and finally the cream.

2 Crumble over the biscuits and serve.

PER POT 229 kcals, protein 3g, carbs 31g, fat 12g, sat fat 6g, fibre 2g, sugar 22g, salt 0.23g

Poached pears in spiced tea

. . . .

Using tea bags to poach fruit saves you having to buy lots of spices or open a bottle of wine.

 25 minutes 4

- 50g/2oz golden caster sugar
- 1 tbsp clear honey
- 1 tbsp redcurrant or cranberry jelly
- 2 spiced-fruit tea bags
- 4 firm pears, peeled, halved and core scooped out with a spoon
- handful fresh cranberries
- natural yogurt or sweetened crème fraîche with a little orange juice or zest, to serve

1 Put the sugar, honey, jelly and tea bags into a big pan with 600ml/1 pint water and bring to the boil, stirring to dissolve the sugar. Add the pear halves, then cover and simmer for 12–15 minutes until the pears are just tender – poke them with a skewer or the tip of a knife to check.

2 Lift out the pears, then turn up the heat, throw in the cranberries and boil for a few minutes until syrupy. Discard the tea bags. Serve the pears with the warm syrup poured over and a spoonful of crème fraîche or yogurt.

. . . .

PER SERVING 131 kcals, protein 1g, carbs 34g, fat none, sat fat none, fibre 4g, sugar 34g, salt 0.02g

Fruity summer Charlotte

Easier than a pie or crumble, but equally delicious. Any sweet or fruit bread will work just as well.

 20 minutes   4

- 500g/1lb 2oz summer fruit (we used raspberries, blackberries and blueberries)
- 4 tbsp demerara sugar
- 7 slices from a small cinnamon and raisin loaf
- 25g/1oz butter, softened
- crème fraîche or fromage frais, to serve

1 Heat oven to 220C/200C fan/gas 7. Tumble three-quarters of the berries into a medium baking dish. Whizz the remaining berries in a food processor to make a purée, then stir this into the dish along with 2 tablespoons of the sugar.

2 Spread the loaf slices with butter, then cut into triangles. Cover the top of the fruit with the bread slices, then scatter with the rest of the sugar. Cover with foil, bake for 10 minutes, uncover the dish, then bake for 5 minutes more until the fruit is starting to bubble and the bread is toasty. Serve with dollops of crème fraîche or fromage frais.

PER SERVING 262 kcals, protein 6g, carbs 47g, fat 7g, sat fat 4g, fibre 5g, sugar 33g, salt 0.43g

Fastest-ever lemon pudding

Just add a scoop of something creamy to this hot, citrusy pud. Ideal on a cold and frosty night.

 15 minutes 4

- 100g/4oz golden caster sugar
- 100g/4oz softened butter
- 100g/4oz self-raising flour
- 2 eggs
- zest 1 lemon
- 1 tsp vanilla extract
- 4 tbsp lemon curd
- crème fraîche or ice cream, to serve

1 Mix the sugar, butter, flour, eggs, lemon zest and vanilla together until creamy, then spoon into a medium microwave-proof baking dish. Microwave on High for 3 minutes, turning halfway through cooking, until risen and set all the way through. Leave to stand for 1 minute.

2 Meanwhile, heat the lemon curd for 30 seconds in the microwave and stir until smooth. Pour all over the top of the pudding and serve with a dollop of crème fraîche or scoops of ice cream.

PER SERVING 457 kcals, protein 6g, carbs 55g, fat 25g, sat fat 14g, fibre 1g, sugar 34g, salt 0.75g

Bakewell trifles

Make these retro cherry-and-almond desserts individually or in a large dish. Either way they are bound to impress.

🕐 15 minutes   🥧 8

- 25g/1oz crunchy amaretti biscuits
- 140g/5oz shop-bought Madeira loaf cake
- ½ x 225g jar cocktail or maraschino cherries, drained, plus extra to decorate
- 200g/8oz cherry compote or jam
- 2 x 150g pots custard
- 300ml/½ pint double cream
- 3 tbsp toasted flaked almonds

1 Crumble the biscuits and cake together into a bowl, roughly mix, then divide among eight small glasses. Halve the cherries and divide among the trifles, then top with compote or jam.

2 Beat together the custard and cream to combine, then dollop on top. Scatter over the almonds, add a cherry half to each trifle and chill until ready to serve.

PER SERVING 415 kcals, protein 4g, carbs 39g, fat 27g, sat fat 14g, fibre 1g, sugar 33g, salt 0.3g

Little iced-lemon mousses

Only four ingredients go into these special little puds, which can either be made ahead or only 30 minutes before you want to eat them.

🕐 30 minutes 🥧 6

- 300–312g jar good-quality lemon curd
- zest 1 lemon
- 300ml pot whipping or double cream
- 25g/1oz lemon shortbread or crunchy lemon-flavoured biscuits, plus extra to serve (optional)

1 Put two-thirds of the lemon curd into a large bowl with the lemon zest and cream, then beat with an electric whisk until it just holds its shape. Dribble over the rest of the lemon curd and divide among six small glass pots or glasses, marbling the curd through as you go. Sit the pots on a small tray, cover the whole lot with cling film and freeze for 20 minutes. (If you want to make these ahead of time just keep them frozen and transfer to the fridge 30 minutes before you want to serve them.)

2 Put the biscuits in a strong plastic bag, if using to decorate, and bash to crumbs with the end of a rolling pin. When you're ready for pudding, remove the pots from the freezer (they should be ice cold but still soft and creamy), top with crumbs and serve with extra biscuits, if you like.

PER MOUSSE 354 kcals, protein 2g, carbs 35g, fat 24g, sat fat 13g, fibre none, sugar 23g, salt 0.14g

Chocolate muffins with hot-chocolate custard

. . . .

A winter warmer the whole family will love, and very easily doubled if the kids have friends over after school.

🕐 20 minutes 🥧 6 ◑ Easily doubled

- 2 tbsp sunflower oil, plus extra for greasing
- 1 tbsp cocoa powder
- 100g/4oz self-raising flour
- ½ tsp bicarbonate of soda
- 50g/2oz golden caster sugar
- 100ml/4fl oz skimmed milk
- 1 egg

FOR THE HOT-CHOCOLATE CUSTARD

- 2 x 150g pots low-fat custard
- 25g/1oz dark chocolate, chopped

1 Heat oven to 180C/160C fan/gas 4. Brush six holes of a muffin tin with a drop of oil. Sieve the cocoa into a large bowl, then add the rest of the dry ingredients. Stir to combine, then make a well in the centre.

2 Beat the milk, egg and oil together in a jug, pour into the well, then stir quickly to make a batter. Spoon into the muffin tin, then bake for 15 minutes or until risen and firm to the touch. Heat the custard in the microwave according to the pack instructions, or in a pan over heat, then tip in the chopped chocolate and stir until smooth. Turn out the muffins into six bowls and pour the custard over.

. . . .

PER SERVING 215 kcals, protein 5g, carbs 32g, fat 8g, sat fat 2g, fibre 1g, sugar 17g, salt 0.59g

Strawberry cheesecakes

· ·

These easy cheesecakes only take minutes to prepare and will probably get eaten in even less time!

🕐 10 minutes, plus chilling   🥧 4

- 85g/3oz low-fat biscuits
- 200g tub extra-light soft cheese
- 200g tub 0% fat Greek yogurt
- 4 tbsp caster sugar
- few drops vanilla extract
- 2 tbsp good-quality strawberry jam
- 100g/4oz strawberries, hulled and sliced

1 Put the biscuits in a plastic bag and bash with a rolling pin until you have chunky crumbs. Divide among four glasses or small bowls.

2 Beat the soft cheese, yogurt, sugar and vanilla together until smooth, then spoon over the crumbs and chill until you are ready to serve.

3 Stir the jam in a bowl until loose, then gently stir in the strawberries. Divide the strawberries among the cheesecakes and serve.

· ·
PER CHEESECAKE 263 kcals, protein 12g, carbs 43g, fat 6g, sat fat 3g, fibre 1g, sugar 31g, salt 0.93g

Apricot French toast

A sweet twist on eggy bread – use whatever fruit is in season. This also makes a great brunch for those with a sweet tooth.

🕐 25 minutes 🥘 4

- 50g/2oz butter
- 6 apricots, halved and stoned
- 200g/8oz caramel sauce
- 350g/12oz ready-made vanilla custard
- 8 small thick slices brioche or white bread, or 4 large slices, halved diagonally

1 Melt 1 tablespoon of the butter in a medium-sized frying pan. Put in the apricots, cut-side down, and gently fry for 2–3 minutes. Flip over and cook for 1 minute more until lightly golden. Add the caramel sauce to the pan and melt until saucy – if it's still too thick to coat the fruit, add a splash of water. Keep in a warm place.

2 Mix the custard with 4 tablespoons water to loosen, then dip in the bread slices, turning to coat thoroughly. Melt half the remaining butter in a large non-stick frying pan. Lightly shake off any excess custard mixture from half the bread slices and fry in the butter for 2 minutes each side until golden. Repeat with the remaining butter and bread, then serve hot, topped with the caramel apricots.

PER SERVING 537 kcals, protein 10g, carbs 77g, fat 24g, sat fat 12g, fibre 3g, sugar 46g, salt 0.94g

Crunchy spiced plums

So easy to make, this pudding will become a real favourite. It has all the elements of a crumble, but none of the hassle.

 25 minutes   4

- 2 tbsp sugar
- 2 whole star anise
- 8 large or 12 small plums, halved
- knob butter
- 4 oaty biscuits (we used Hobnobs)
- custard or vanilla ice cream, to serve

1 Heat oven to 200C/180C fan/gas 6. Mix the sugar with 2 tablespoons water in a baking dish, add the star anise, then pop in the plums, cut-side down. They should fit quite snugly. Dot with the butter. Roast for about 5 minutes until the plums are starting to soften on the bottom, then turn them over. Roast for another 5 minutes or until tender – this will depend on how ripe your fruit is.

2 Roughly crush the biscuits, then spoon a little on top of each plum half. Return to the oven for a few minutes more until the biscuit topping takes on a dark gold colour. Serve the plums and their scented, syrupy juices with custard or ice cream.

PER SERVING 169 kcals, protein 2g, carbs 31g, fat 5g, sat fat 2g, fibre 3g, sugar 25g, salt 0.18g

Index

Also available from BBC Books and Good Food